Jenny Wren

Dawn L. Watkins

journey**forth**®

Greenville, South Carolina

Jenny Wren
Dawn L. Watkins

Edited by Carolyn Cooper
Designed by Nathan Hutcheon
Cover and illustrations by Stephanie True

© 1986 by BJU Press
Greenville, South Carolina 29614
JourneyForth Books is a division of BJU Press

ISBN 978-0-89084-324-6

20   19

Dedicated to
Sarah

Contents

1

THE NEW PLACE

The sudden perking sound of a tractor starting woke Jenny. The first thing she saw was an airy curtain lifting lightly on an August morning breeze. She heard the tractor settle into an even chugging, and then she remembered where she was.

It usually took her a month to get used to a new place, to get so she would know where she was as soon as she woke up. Somehow this place had not been as hard for her as the other places.

On the wall at the end of the bed was a photograph in a wooden frame. It was of a man, a woman, and four children sitting on a porch. Jenny looked at the picture every morning, and every morning she wondered what it was like to belong to a family like that.

Jenny slipped out of bed and looked out the window, through the heavy green hemlocks, toward the barn. A red tractor, hung with great chains and logging tools, moved slowly up the road past the milkhouse.

As she started to get dressed, a pleasant voice called up through the round grating in the floor beside the bed.

"Are you up, Jenny?" the woman's voice asked.

Jenny kneeled by the grating. She could see the white enamel wood stove below and hear dishes rattling in the sink off to the right. At first the hole in the floor with its iron covering had seemed odd to Jenny. Now it was familiar.

"Yes, just now," she called back.

"Come on down, then, and get some breakfast."

Jenny buttoned her shirt, brushed her long, brown hair, and meandered downstairs. When she opened the stair door into the kitchen, she expected Lady, the big gold collie, to be there, but she wasn't.

"Good morning, Jenny," said a short, gray-haired woman in a calico apron. "Do you want an egg for breakfast?"

"Yes, please," answered Jenny, looking around a little for the collie.

"All right. Go wash your face," said the woman. With a twinkle in her eye she added, "Lady's out with Grandpa. If you hurry, you can catch them."

As Jenny ate the scrambled egg, the woman made two braids of Jenny's hair. "Can't have your hair all loose if you're going logging with Grandpa."

"Maybe Mr. Logan doesn't want me along," said Jenny, ignoring the swift, neat braiding going on just over her right ear.

"Why, sure he does. I think he even waited around a little this morning, just in case you woke up. So you hurry up and brush your teeth and foot it up the hill there."

"Mrs. Logan?" said Jenny as the stocky little woman slipped a band around the end of the braid.

"Call me Grandma, can't you?" The woman looked nearly the same as she had in the photograph, except for her hair.

"Are you sure I don't get in the way?"

"I'm sure, Jenny. Now scoot."

At first Jenny ran along the road up past the barn and the corn crib. Then the road became two bare tracks through wispy grass. The hay was still wet with dew and the brown-eyed susans hadn't fully lifted their heads to the sun. She passed a level place at the bottom of the mountain where Mr. Logan kept his huge circular saw. To the left was the Logans' old workhorse, browsing in his pasture. Jenny paused a second to watch him. As she started up the steep field, she remembered to swing her foot in front of her, pulling the grass over and down, to watch for snakes. Usually she walked behind Mr. Logan, and that was how he did it.

The tractor was nearly to the woods before the white-haired driver in a gray work shirt noticed Jenny following him. Without a word, he stopped the tractor and waved for her to come on. She ran up the tracks the huge wheels had crushed through the grass, stepped on the hitch, and pulled herself up to stand against the wheel shield on Mr. Logan's left. Mr.

Logan let the brake out and they moved forward with a lurch. After a while, Mr. Logan called over the noise of the tractor.

"Did you have any breakfast?"

"An egg and orange juice."

He nodded.

Soon they entered the woods, the narrow logging road weaving through thick ferns ahead. Jenny glimpsed Lady bounding after something in the underbrush.

"Will Lady get lost?" she yelled to the driver.

"Doubtful," he answered.

The way got steeper. The tractor joggled its riders about but kept climbing. Branches of witch hazel hung out over the road here and there, forcing the old man and the little girl to duck. Sometimes Mr. Logan held the branch up until they went under; sometimes Jenny did.

The last part of the climb seemed almost straight up to Jenny. She had come with Mr. Logan several times in the past three weeks, but this part still scared her. The tractor seemed barely to move, grinding up the steep path. Sometimes it was as if the big machine hung between falling and climbing, churning the soft, dark earth of the forest. But every time they made it to the top, and every time Jenny forgot she had been afraid.

The top of the mountain was flat with great tall trees as far as she could see. Jenny thought of herself as a visitor and the trees as the owners of the place. The trees went up, straight and smooth, until at the very top, their thick branches and rich leaves reached up and out. Slanting shafts of sun shot down through the towering oaks, dappling the laurel and ferns below. In each beam, Jenny could see a misty dust swirling slowly by. Nowhere, thought Jenny, could anything be as beautiful. She wondered what it might be like to be a tree and always have your head up on the edge of the world, looking out at the sun.

Mr. Logan shut off the tractor and set the brake. Then he just sat, listening to the stillness pour in around them as the tractor noise died. In the distance Jenny heard the hollow drumming that she now recognized as a woodpecker at work. Birds that are heard only in the woods were whistling and twittering above them. Once in a while the hot engine ticked as it settled into silence. The air was cool and smelled of leaves and ferns, and damp earth. Lady appeared and lay down under the tractor, putting her head forward on her front paws.

Mr. Logan got down from his seat and pulled his axe out of its holder. Every sound seemed loud in the woods, and Jenny always felt as if she should whisper at first. She sat in the tractor seat and watched Mr. Logan walk through the laurel to the fallen trees. He was the biggest man Jenny had ever seen; he seemed like one of the trees. He swung his axe against a branch of a tree that lay on the ground. The whack she heard first, then its quick echo. A chip flew up, and Mr. Logan pulled his axe free. Again he brought it down and the branch let go with a ripping sound.

Jenny Wren

"Mr. Logan?"

"What?" he answered, straightening up to look at her.

"Is it all right to get down now?"

"I guess. But keep where you can see the tractor, and watch for snakes."

She nimbly swung down and high-stepped through the ferns to where he was working. She dragged the branch to the brush pile and waited for him to cut another away from the tree. Then she went up and pulled it to the pile. Between trips she looked at the leaves on the twigs, the toadstools, and the moss.

"Look at this tiny tree," she exclaimed.

The big man leaned forward.

"Yep. A little pine. There are a lot in here if you look around. Someday this will be all pine," he said as he made a sweep with his free hand.

"When?"

He gave a little laugh. "Well, not till you're older than I am anyway." Then he turned back to his chopping.

All morning they worked together and talked only a little. Finally he thumped his axe into a log and said, "Let's see if Chippie is around today."

Chippie was a chipmunk they fed every day at a big pine by the stream.

Sometimes he didn't come at all and sometimes he was waiting for them. This time he was waiting, flicking his tail and scrambling around the roots of the tree. Mr. Logan pulled a few kernels of corn from his overalls pocket and gave them to Jenny. She threw them under the tree, and Chippie pounced forward. Grabbing up a kernel, he whisked away through the ferns.

"Where does he go?" she asked.

"To his house, maybe, to put the corn away."

"Does every animal have a home?"

"I guess so." He stood with his arms crossed, smiling a little.

Jenny waited, and soon the chipmunk returned, darting part way up the tree trunk and then zipping down to get another kernel.

"How did this pine get here?" asked Jenny, remembering the small pines at the clearing.

"This is a grandfather tree. See how crooked it is and how knobby and big the roots? It's been here a long time, since when this forest was mostly pine."

"Do the trees take turns owning the woods?"

Mr. Logan gave a short chuckle. "Well, I guess you could say that."

"How come this pine tree is still here, then?" she asked.

"Well, because it's right here on the stream, I guess."

Chippie had collected all the kernels and was not coming back. Mr. Logan strode back through the underbrush with Jenny right on his heels.

"Suppose Grandma will be wanting us back for dinner," he said over his shoulder. He picked up the axe without stopping and headed for the tractor. Jenny ran ahead, to get Lady out of the way.

"Get up, Lady," she called. Lady stretched awake and shoved out from under the wheels. "Come out of the way." Lady strolled over to Jenny to be petted, but Jenny never petted her in the woods. The dog seemed different to Jenny among the tall trees, and she only wanted to be sure the dog didn't get run over.

"Don't hit Lady," Jenny said loudly near Mr. Logan's ear as the tractor started up.

"She'll look out," was the only answer.

Going down, the tractor rumbled and lumbered about, its stack sending out gray and white smoke. Jenny could feel the warmth of the smoke against her cheeks once in a while. On the narrow, steep grades it seemed as if they must surely tip over. Jenny closed her eyes and hung on, afraid to look and afraid not to. Soon the tractor chugged along less desperately, and Jenny saw they were nearly to the field. When they left the woods, they could see rolling farmland for miles in both directions. And straight ahead down in the valley, Jenny could see the top of the red roof on the Logans' farmhouse.

She pointed toward the red patch, and the old woodsman nodded with one of his slight smiles.

In the kitchen was chicken soup and johnny cakes. The table was set, and the clock on the shelf was chiming a quarter past twelve.

"About time you showed up," Mrs. Logan said, with pretended sternness. "Thought I was going to have to ring the dinner bell."

"Chippie was slow today," said the man.

Jenny pulled up the chair that she had been told was hers and took a drink of milk.

"Better wait for the blessing," said Mr. Logan.

"That's right," Mrs. Logan said firmly, without turning from the stove.

Mr. Logan scrunched up his shoulders, tucked his head, and opened his eyes in mock alarm. Jenny smiled a little.

"Jenny, can you carry one of these bowls?" Mrs. Logan asked.

To the stove in a flash, Jenny received a heavy blue and white soup plate, filled almost too full. She carried it slowly, evenly, to the table and put it down by bending her knees rather than by lowering her arms. It seemed safer that way.

Mr. Logan said the blessing. Jenny looked from the old man to the old woman during the prayer. There had been others who said blessings over their meals; Jenny had even memorized some of the prayers, she had heard them so often. But these people annoyed her sometimes. They prayed as if they were talking to someone right there. And she particularly disliked it when they prayed for her.

"And, Lord, make us thankful for all you send us," the man was saying. "Amen."

Jenny was always careful to close her eyes before the *amen*.

After dinner, Mr. Logan drank a glass of thick buttermilk. He offered some to Jenny, but she didn't like the way it looked.

"How's your new help working out?" Mrs. Logan asked Mr. Logan.

"Just dandy. I've got the best branch-trimmer in the business."

Jenny looked away and pretended not to hear what they had said. She stroked Lady's silky head and put her cheek against the thick fur of the dog's neck.

"You're pretty glad to get her, I guess," said Mrs. Logan.

"She'll do," the old man said, sitting down in his rocker by the open window. Jenny knew he would sit there in the breeze for twenty minutes or so. She went outside to wait. Shortly she heard his step on the porch. She looked up at him, but he did not look at her.

"I have to put gas in the tractor. That will give you time to help Grandma clear the table, won't it?" Then he went down the steps and out toward the barn.

Jenny was embarrassed and went in to clear the table. Gathering up the dishes was the one chore she had trouble remembering to do. She carried the dishes to the sink and stacked them. The tractor started up. Jenny went and sat in the rocker.

"Grandpa's leaving, Jenny," Mrs. Logan said.

"I don't want to go," she mumbled.

"You don't?" asked Mrs. Logan, truly surprised. "Why not?"

"Because he doesn't like me."

"Doesn't like you? Well, I guess he *does*. What makes you talk like that?" Mrs. Logan leaned back from the sink to look at Jenny.

Jenny was silent.

Mrs. Logan started to draw the dishwater. "Go tell him that you're not going, then, so he doesn't wait."

Jenny walked out to the tractor rather slowly. Mr. Logan added a big chain to the ones already on the back.

"Ready to go?" he looked up, pleasantly.

She had expected him to be angry at her for forgetting to do her job. Now it was too hard to explain why she didn't want to go.

"Just a minute," she said.

She ran back to the porch and called through the screen door.

"I'm going on the mountain."

"Suit yourself," came the half-amused answer.

That afternoon, Lady sat under the tractor and Jenny sat on it, watching Mr. Logan.

When he felled trees, Jenny was not allowed to get down. "I want to know exactly where you are," was all he had said when Jenny had asked why she had to stay on the tractor.

Mr. Logan studied each tree before he cut it down, marking each one where he would begin chopping it. Sometimes he would turn to Jenny and point with his axe which way the tree was going to fall. She would nod back. Then he would draw back his axe and begin the chopping, every swing thwacking solidly against the trunk. Chips would fly away by the axe head, and the smaller branches would quiver slightly. In a while, not long it seemed to Jenny, the tree would begin to creak and then slowly, slowly begin to lean. Mr. Logan would take a step back, watching the tree tip more and more forward. The great tree would at first hesitate, tottering between earth and sky, and then suddenly give way with a great sweeping rush and come crashing level against the forest floor. Sometimes a tree would bounce as it hit, and the limber branches would seem to swell and drop back like a green wave. But the trees always fell right where Mr. Logan had said they would.

Late in the afternoon the old woodsman laid out the heavy chains and rolled the trimmed logs onto them. Then he hooked the chains around the three biggest logs and bolted the chains to the tractor hitch. It was hot work; he pulled out his big handkerchief several times to wipe his face. Finally he drew out his pocket watch and looked at it.

"Time to get the cows in," he said. "Better go."

They pulled the logs behind the tractor. Jenny watched them plowing up the dirt and rolling against each other. Lady followed behind the logs, and Jenny worried she might get squeezed between them, but the dog had done this many times before and was careful.

At the bottom of the mountain, they undid the chains and left the logs beside the big saw. When they got to the barn, Mr. Logan parked the tractor and gathered the chains.

"Can you open the gate while Lady gets the cows?" he asked.

Jenny jumped down.

"Bring the cows home," she called, and Lady trotted out to the pasture.

Then Jenny pushed up the wide wooden latch and ran with the heavy gate to open it.

Soon she saw the nine cows coming over the small rise behind the barn, with Lady ever at their heels. Jenny climbed up the fence to watch and be out of the way. She had a comfortable feeling inside when it was time for the cows to come in, sort of safe and lazy.

The cows filed through the gate and up to their own stanchions.

"How do they know which place is whose?" she had asked the first time she had seen them come in.

"Well," Mr. Logan had answered, "They just get used to having their own places. Then they just remember, I guess."

"Do they ever get mixed up?"

"Only if some new cow gets in the wrong place."

"Then what happens?" she asked.

"I lead the new girl in for a few days 'til she knows where to go."

"Then everything's okay after that?"

"Yep. Everything's okay."

Mr. Logan went down the line, snapping the chains of the stanchions to the halters on the cows.

Then he took a pail and a stool and milked each cow by hand. Jenny went with him, watching intently.

"Want to try?" he asked.

"Oh no." She backed away. He chuckled.

He was nearly finished with his chores when Jenny asked him a question.

"Mr. Logan, how do the trees know whose turn it is to own the forest?"

He looked at her over his shoulder.

"How's that?"

"You know, the pines and the oaks, they take turns owning the forest."

"Oh," he said. Turning back to his milking, he took his time.

"Well, how do they?" she asked again after a while.

"Let me think about that one," he said.

As they put the cows out, Jenny saw old Benjamin, the great work horse, high in the pasture. She was afraid of him up close, but far away he was beautiful.

"Why do you keep Benjamin?"

"Because he worked hard for me many years, and we're old friends," the farmer replied.

How could anyone be friends with a big horse like that, she wondered.

Lady, Mr. Logan, and Jenny turned toward the farmhouse. There was already a light on in the kitchen. And, they saw as they rounded the corner, there was a strange car in the driveway.

2

THE STOVEPIPE HOLE

As Jenny entered the kitchen, a man in a suit and a pretty woman stood up.

"Nicholas," said Mrs. Logan, "these people have come to see Jenny."

"Mr. Logan," said the man, stepping forward, "I'm John Wright, and this is Gayle Paterson."

Jenny smelled ham and potatoes, and she saw that the table was set for three.

"Sorry to get here at mealtime, but we got lost looking for your place. We won't hold you up long," the man went on.

"I offered supper," said Mrs. Logan to her husband, "but they're in a hurry."

"What can we do for you?" said Mr. Logan. He hung his cap on a peg by the door and strolled over to the table and pulled out the end chair. As he sat down, Miss Paterson took back the rocker, and Mr. Wright sat again in the desk chair, somewhat stiffly.

"Well," said Miss Paterson, speaking to Mr. Logan, but smiling on Jenny, "we want to know how Jenny's getting along."

Everyone waited for Jenny to speak. When she said nothing, Mr. Logan answered.

"She seems to be doing fine. Makes a good logger." He winked at Jenny.

She still stood sullenly by the door, holding Lady by the collar.

"Are you from the welfare?" she asked abruptly.

"That's right," said the man.

"Where's Mrs. McAllister?"

"She's on vacation. But she'll be back before school starts." He turned to Mr. Logan. "Which is why we're here. We're trying to find a place for Jenny before school starts."

"Why, can't she go to school here? We have a fine school right out to the crossroads here," said Nicholas Logan, showing the direction with his hand.

"I know the school, sir, and I'm sure it's a good one. But that's not the point. Jenny's staying with you was just a temporary thing—until we could find her another place."

"That's what you said. But we have plenty of room, and I think Jenny likes it here. Don't you, Eda?" said Nicholas to his wife.

"Maybe we should ask Jenny," said Mrs. Logan.

Jenny had slumped down beside the cupboard and was stroking Lady's head.

"It's okay," she said without looking up.

Mr. Wright smiled slightly. "We're pretty sure we have a place near here even. Out in Mileston. You could even visit Jenny once in a while." He smiled a little more broadly and looked from Mrs. Logan to Mr. Logan.

Mr. Logan laid his arm on the kitchen table and looked directly at Mr. Wright. "What you mean to say is that we're too old in your book."

Mr. Wright laughed an embarrassed laugh. "Now, Mr. Logan, what I mean to say is that when you took Jenny in last month, we only wanted to let her stay in the area until we found another home for her." He looked at Miss Paterson. "It was somewhat irregular, even at that."

Miss Paterson looked at him, puzzled.

"You see," he explained, "the wife where Jenny was staying had to take in her sister who had been in an accident, and there was no room for Jenny. The Logans, being neighbors, offered to keep Jenny a while."

All the time, Jenny sat cross-legged by the cupboard, neither smiling nor frowning.

"Can you be ready next Thursday, Jenny? You'll want to get settled before school starts," said Mr. Wright.

"Sure," answered the girl, looking steadily at him.

"Who in Mileston?" asked Mr. Logan, simply.

"John and Sally . . . Stebbs, I believe the name is."

"They've kept a good many children, haven't they?" said Mrs. Logan.

"Yes, they have."

"Well," said Miss Paterson, "these people have been kept from their meal long enough. We'd better be going."

"Yes. Thank you, Mr. Logan, Mrs. Logan. We'll be in touch. And I'll see you next Thursday, Jenny."

The couple left, and Mr. Logan came back in from the porch and sat in the rocker by the stove. The steady tick of the clock was the only sound for a long time.

Finally he said, "Is supper ruined, Eda?"

"I doubt it," she said, rising. "Shall we eat?"

"Well, I'm hungry, aren't you, Jenny?"

"Sure," said Jenny, without expression.

Supper was quiet. Jenny felt a little sorry for the old couple.

"Don't worry about me," she said.

"We're not," the old man said.

"How much milk tonight?" asked Mrs. Logan.

"A goodly sum. Millie's about the best cow we ever had."

"Are you going to sell it all to Jacob in the morning?" the wife asked.

"Yep."

"Thought I might make a little butter, if we kept the cream."

Mr. Logan made no answer.

After supper, Mrs. Logan and Jenny did the dishes. All the while, they played a number game.

"What are three nines?" inquired the old lady.

"Twenty-seven."

"And five sevens?"

"Thirty-five."

"Good. What's six plus four?"

"Ten."

"And five plus seven minus two?"

"That's hard."

"Five plus seven minus two."

There was a short pause. "Ten."

"Why, you're a whiz, Jenny!"

"Let's spell a while," said the girl.

"All right. Do you remember how to spell *chrysanthemum?*" said Mrs. Logan, looking out of the corner of her eye at Jenny.

"C-h-r-y-s-a-n-t-h-e-m-u-m."

"Very good! And *secretary?*"

"S-e-c-r-a-t-a-r-y."

"No, you missed that one. One letter wrong."

"How is it?"

"S-e-c-r-*e*-t-a-r-y," said Mrs. Logan, stressing the second *e*.

"Teach me another long one like *chrysanthemum*."

"Spell *secretary* first."

"S-e-c-r-*e*-t-a-r-y," said Jenny, stressing the *e*. Mrs. Logan smiled and nodded.

"How about learning *refrigerator?*"

"Okay," said Jenny.

"All right. How does it sound like it might be spelled?"

After the dishes, Mrs. Logan did a crossword puzzle. Jenny played one game of checkers with Mr. Logan. They played on a tall, narrow table built especially to be a checkerboard. "Now, Jenny, you're not watching. You have a jump."

"Where?"

"You look for it. It's enough I told you there was one."

"Is this it?" she asked, pointing to a red checker.

"Well, is it?" he asked her.

She picked up the checker and took the jump. He watched her remove his black checker before he spoke.

"Look here." And he jumped two red checkers. "If you had jumped this way," he said, pointing, "I couldn't have gotten any of your men. You have to watch."

Jenny sat back in her chair. "You're too good. I can't beat you."

"You'll get it pretty soon," he said.

"About finished with your game?" asked Mrs. Logan, folding up the crossword puzzle.

"Yes," Jenny replied, forlornly.

"We'll try again tomorrow," said the big man, leaning forward in his rocker to collect the checkers. "You just need more practice."

Mrs. Logan opened her Bible on the kitchen table. Jenny had gotten used to this evening ritual, but she still didn't like it. The clock ticked, the rocker squeaked, the thin Bible pages rattled. Suddenly Jenny felt sleepy and bored.

"Nehemiah. Chapter two. 'And it came to pass in the month Nisan, in the twentieth year of Artaxerxes the king, that wine was before him: and I took up the wine, and gave it unto the king. Now I had not been beforetime sad in his presence.

"'Wherefore the king said unto me, Why is thy countenance sad, seeing thou art not sick? this is nothing else but sorrow of heart. Then was I very sore afraid,

"'And said unto the king, Let the king live for ever: why should not my countenance be sad, when the city, the place of my fathers' sepulchres, lieth waste, and the gates thereof are consumed with fire?

"'Then the king said unto me, For what dost thou make request? So I prayed to the God of heaven.

"'And I said unto the king, If it please the king, and if thy servant have found favour in thy sight, that thou wouldest send me unto Judah, unto the city of my fathers' sepulchres, that I may build it.'"

Mrs. Logan read on to the end of the chapter.

"Mrs. Logan," said Jenny sleepily, "was Nehemiah homesick?"

"I guess you might say that," she answered with a little laugh.

"Why was he? Was the king mean to him?"

"I don't think so. Nehemiah knew there was a job to do at home, and he wanted to be there." She looked over at Mr. Logan. "You two have had a hard day."

"Yep," he said. "We better hit the hay."

"Get a shower, Jenny. Your nightgown's in the bathroom."

When she came back, Mrs. Logan said, as always, "Let me see your neck. And the bottoms of your feet. Pretty good. Want a cookie or a piece of toast?"

"No, thank you."

"Okay, then, brush your teeth. And be a bit quicker. We want to get to bed too."

The clock struck nine. Jenny padded back to the kitchen.

"Can Lady sleep in my room?"

"Too hot for dogs upstairs tonight," said the old gentleman. "She'll be better off out on the porch. Here, girl."

Lady ambled out to the porch. Mr. Logan locked the door.

Jenny received a hug and a kiss from the aproned wife without comment.

"Good night, honey. Sleep tight. Shall I come along and get the light?"

"No. I can get it."

Mrs. Logan looked at her gently but did not argue.

"Didn't anyone ever tuck you in, child?"

Jenny did not answer.

"Jenny," said Mr. Logan, "do you like it here?"

"Yes. It's fine."

"Would you want to stay here?"

"I can't." She tied the little bow on the neck of her nightgown.

"If you could."

"Yes, I guess so."

He looked kindly down at her. "I'm sorry you get moved around so much."

She opened the stair door. "It doesn't matter. Good night." Then she went up.

As she pulled back the covers, she could hear the Logans' voices coming up through the register in the floor.

Carefully, quietly, she edged over in the darkness and kneeled by the grating. She could see part of the rocker and half of the stove. Mr. Logan was standing in front of the rocker.

"What about the cream, Nicholas?" Mrs. Logan was saying.

"Well, I'll tell you," he said, lifting a stove lid and tipping it slightly for the night. "If it is a clear day tomorrow, we'll keep it for butter. If it's raining in the morning, so I can't cut wood, we'll make a little trip over to Mileston—to see John and Sally."

"I thought we might," she said as she stepped over to him and threw a piece of paper in the stove. "Think that'll change anything?"

"Might. Say, do you know why pines can take over a forest when there haven't been any for years?"

"Not right off," she said with a little smile.

"I don't either. But I need to find out."

"Why?"

"I just need to know, woman."

Then he leaned over and gave her a kiss.

Upstairs, in the darkness, Jenny blushed.

3

A DISMAL DAY

It was not raining the next morning, but it was cloudy. Jenny was up earlier than usual. She was downstairs before Mr. Logan had come in from milking.

"After breakfast," Mrs. Logan told her, "I want you to go back upstairs and put on a dress—the plaid one with the white collar. We're going visiting."

"But it's not raining," said Jenny before she thought.

"It will be," replied Mrs. Logan, lifting a piece of wood from the wood box. She straightened up and looked at Jenny. "You wouldn't have been listening through the stovepipe hole, would you?" She put the wood in the stove. "Eavesdroppers usually hear things they wish they hadn't, you know."

She laid the lid-lifter on the shelf above the range. "I want to heat the oven now in case the day gets too hot later on. Can you bring a couple sticks in from the wood box on the porch?"

Jenny went out. Mr. Logan and Lady were coming from the barn. Jenny waited for them, not wanting to hear any more from Mrs. Logan about eavesdropping. She was used to being yelled at, and she preferred it. These quiet ways of correction embarrassed her.

"Good morning, Jenny Wren," said the old man as he strode onto the porch. "Up early, aren't you?"

"I can get up early if anybody calls me," she said with a little temper. "I'm not lazy!"

"Sounds as if you got up a bit *too* early," he answered simply and passed by her to the kitchen.

In the car, Jenny sat in the back seat, watching the countryside slide past. It began to rain, and big drops drizzled down the window. Woodlands, open meadows, pastures went by beyond the glazed window beside her. The cows, barns, and farmhouses thinned out, and later—it seemed a long time to Jenny—a gas station appeared, then a few stores, then more and more houses, many of them one-story with neat lawns about the size of Mrs. Logan's kitchen. Some houses had fences around them, others had hedges. It was raining steadily now and getting chilly.

They pulled into the driveway of one of these houses; it was a narrow drive but smoothly paved. Lined with yellow and lavender flowers, the short walk led up to a porch without rails.

"No umbrella, women," laughed Mr. Logan. "We'll have to make a run for it."

He put on his Stetson; Mrs. Logan threw a scarf over her head. Jenny didn't care if her braids got wet. Together they hurried to the porch.

The door was soon opened by a woman with short, curly black hair. Her eyes brightened when she saw the Logans.

"Why, Nicholas and Eda! Come in out of the weather! Let me take your hat, Nicholas. Oh, don't mind your shoes. Come in, come in. And who is this?" she asked, smiling fully on Jenny.

"Jenny. She's been staying with us for a while," replied the handsome farmer, handing over his hat.

"Hello, Jenny. I'm Sally. There are some children here I think you'll like to meet."

Jenny could hear a television in the other room and girls laughing.

"Nicholas, Eda, have a seat, and I'll be right back. Now, then, Jenny, what's your last name?"

"Star."

"Star?" Sally looked back at Mr. Logan with a puzzled expression.

"Well, you come with me and meet the others. I think you're in time to get in on the Monopoly game. We play that around here when it rains all day."

Jenny went along without saying anything. The family room was full of toys, and the television blared in the corner.

"Lynn, please turn down the television and come meet Jenny."

Lynn did so, politely.

"And this is Teresa," said the woman, nodding toward the other, older girl. "Jenny is visiting, so you be hospitable now."

After she left, Lynn asked, "Do you want to play Monopoly?"

"No, thank you."

Teresa and Lynn sat silent for a while and then began their game again.

Jenny drifted toward the door and stood looking into the living room at the Logans. Mr. Logan wore a starched light blue dress shirt that made his hair look very white and his eyes very blue. Mrs. Logan had on the maroon gingham dress she wore to the grocery store. Jenny thought the couple looked good together.

"I know," Mr. Logan was saying, "but I thought I might ask you and John to help. Where is John, anyway?"

"He should be back soon. Went downtown this morning. Can I get you some coffee or tea?"

"No, thank you. We just ate," said Mrs. Logan. "We know it's rather early to be calling, but Nicholas has a lot of wood to get in yet."

"Might be an early fall," he said. "The thing is," he went on, getting back to his main concern, "I don't know how this system works. For keeping children, I mean. Eda and I want Jenny to stay where she is. How do we do that?"

"She's supposed to come here, you know."

"We know," said Mrs. Logan. "And it's not that we don't think you're fine people—why, my lands, just look at all the children you've taken in. It's just that Jenny has moved around too much. And she needs one place to call home."

"That's the thing," said Mr. Logan. "She doesn't get attached to anything or anybody. No wonder—having to leave place after place. She's got to stay put, or she's going to grow up without heart."

Jenny's interest quickened, and she leaned forward slightly.

"Well, I've seen a lot of kids like that," said Sally Stebbs. "Mostly, they only pretend not to care. But about your keeping Jenny, I don't know. There's a lot going against it." She looked up, kindly, and paused.

"Too old, huh?" said Mr. Logan.

"Well, they like young people, you know. How old are you, if you don't mind my asking?"

"Sixty-six. Eda's sixty-two. Don't they make any exceptions for special cases?"

"Sometimes. But then there's another thing. Jenny has an emotional problem."

"The only thing wrong with her is that she's afraid to believe in anything or anybody," Mrs. Logan said.

Mrs. Stebbs nodded. "She's been in three homes that I know of. Her parents just gave her over, I guess."

"Oh," Mrs. Logan said softly. "I just can't understand how they could."

Mrs. Stebbs sort of snorted. "Well, people do. Anyway, there's just more going against your keeping her than you maybe know about."

"We knew she was not doing so well in school," Mr. Logan said. "But she's coming around a little, and I can see she's real quick."

Jenny felt her heart jump at his words. She had never thought of herself as smart.

"Why, yes," said Mrs. Logan. "Jenny could do fine in school if she had a place—a sure place—to call home."

Jenny stepped back into the playroom. "Without heart," she repeated to herself. What did he mean by that? She sat down in front of the television. A cowboy was swinging a lasso and riding a black horse at a gallop. "I have a heart," she thought sullenly.

A long time later, Mrs. Stebbs came to the doorway. "Time to go, Jenny. Did you have a good time? Who won the game?"

"Jenny didn't play," said Lynn. "She watched television."

"I see," said the lady. "Well, you must come again and get in on the game."

All the way to the Logans', Jenny stared at the back of the seat. She had heard many people say she had "an emotional problem." But she had never heard she was "without heart."

Mr. Logan put the car away as Mrs. Logan and Jenny walked to the house. It was only drizzling now.

"Am I polite?" Jenny suddenly asked.

"Most of the time, sugar."

"Am I a bother?"

"Not a bit." The lady smiled down at her.

Jenny wanted to ask if she had a heart, but she thought better of it. Instead she said, "What would you do to me if I were?"

Mrs. Logan studied the face turned up to her. "Why? Are you making plans to be one?" she asked with a gentle smile.

"No," Jenny replied, seriously.

"Well, good. Because I would have to say, 'Jenny, you must stop being a bother!'"

Lady stood up and stretched, first forward then behind. She came forward, wagging and sniffing.

"Did you miss us, Lady?" asked the farmer's wife, unlocking the door. "Cools right off in here when it rains. I'm glad I made that little fire this morning. Shall I make a pie for supper?"

"If you want," said Jenny as she went up to change her clothes.

That afternoon Jenny tried to learn how to crochet. Mrs. Logan showed her again and again how to hold the hook and how to turn her hand. What Mrs. Logan made was smooth and straight. What Jenny made was lumpy and looped.

"I can't do it."

"All you need is more patience and more practice," Mrs. Logan said.

"What are you going to make?"

"A rug."

"Will it take long?"

"Well, it won't be done by supper, that's sure."

The radio played cheerily. Jenny looked around the sitting room. The cuckoo clock pendulum swung back and forth on the wall beside the sofa. Suddenly the door on the clock sprang open, and the cuckoo thrust out his head and cuckooed once.

"But it's three o'clock," Jenny said.

"He can't tell time very well, can he?"

"How come we never sit in this room?"

"We do in the winter. A nice big fire in the fireplace there. Evenings are longer then, you know. Not so much work to do."

The walls were a rich beige; the ceiling was white. A carved piece of dark wood ran along the top of the walls where they met the ceiling. Jenny looked down at the huge tapestry rug that nearly covered the whole floor and studied the design. Then she went over and stood in front of a giant fern which sat by a window that framed the farm down the road.

"Why do you like me?" she asked at length.

"Why shouldn't I?" Mrs. Logan put down her work.

"Why do you, though?"

"Because you're a sweet little thing."

"You don't even know me." Jenny turned around.

"Sure I do."

"No, you don't. Nobody knows me." Jenny felt her temper coming up, and even she was surprised.

"Is that right? Well, suppose you tell me who you are, and then I'll know."

"I'm going out to the barn," she said.

"Pull the kitchen door to as you leave," said Mrs. Logan, crocheting again in a steady rhythm.

Jenny found Mr. Logan hammering and sawing up on the barn floor.

He looked up as she walked past him but said nothing. She opened the granary door. It was always clean and dry in the granary. The bin was half full of oats. Plunging her hands deep into the oats, she pulled out two fistfuls of grain. As she slowly opened her hands, the grains trickled down into the bin, rolled over and over, and settled against the wooden sides. A dim light fell through the small, high window and spread over the grain and the baskets by the door. On the opposite wall hung the heavy leather harness that Benjamin used to wear.

She went over and ran her hand along the reins. The straps, shiny and smooth, ticked against the wall as she touched them. The chains farther back chinked a little. The smell of the oats and the leather filled her nostrils. There was something vastly settled and pleasant about the granary. It always looked freshly swept, old, quiet.

Out on the barn floor, the saw rasped back and forth, back and forth. Then with a little crackling sound, a piece of wood gave way and dropped with a muted thud on the plank floor. As Jenny came out of the granary, she saw Mr. Logan hold a long strip of wood out in front of him and look with one eye down its length.

"What are you doing?" she asked, from a distance.

"I'm making a surprise for Grandma."

"What is it?"

"It's a surprise. So don't you tell you saw me out here, will you?"

"No."

He smiled at her. Jenny determined to keep the secret.

She watched from a seat she had made of a grain sack. Slowly, carefully, he planed the wood, turning each piece again and again, studying all the angles with an expert eye.

"This is curly maple. I've been saving it for a long time. Work on it when I can."

Jenny said nothing. In a little while, she lost interest in the work and went down the stairs to where the cows came to be milked. Soon it would be time for them to come in, and she would watch them come over the hill.

The barn was so quiet when it was empty that she thought of it as almost a different building. In the dampness, the straw and hay smelled thick and musty. It was dim between the stanchions and nearly dark in the stalls. Overhead Jenny could see the mud nests of swallows plastered to the huge beams.

In the corner of one window, a spider was making a web. She spent a long time watching the intricate process, being careful not to get too close to the spider. After a while she went outside and around to the same window to watch the spider from the other side. Putting her hands against the gray, weathered wood, she leaned forward and looked up at the spider, which was slowly letting itself down

by a shiny thread. And then all at once she became aware of her reflection in the bespeckled barn window. She stared at her own smooth cheeks and loosely braided hair. It seemed as if her eyes were larger than she had thought of them as being. She stepped back from the window, still looking at her reflection, but feeling as if she had seen someone else staring back at her from inside the barn.

"You didn't eat much supper, honey," said Mrs. Logan after supper. "Don't you like dumplings?"

"They're okay."

"Do you feel all right?" asked Mrs. Logan, picking up Jenny's pie plate.

"Yes."

Mrs. Logan bent over her and gave her a hug. Jenny sat still. "Don't hug me."

The old lady pulled back but made no comment. She scraped a few dishes onto a plate, then carried them all to the sink. She drew the dishwater and started to wash the glasses.

"Was that very nice, Jenny?" Mr. Logan asked.

She answered nothing.

"You've been in a foul humor most all day. I'm ashamed of you. There is never any excuse for being nasty. I won't have it." His voice was low, even, and calm. But his mouth was set, his eyes direct.

She dried the dishes in silence.

"You had a pretty dull day, didn't you?" asked Mrs. Logan.

"It was okay."

"If it rains again tomorrow, we'll go up in the attic and get some books for you. There must be some up there from when the kids were little."

Jenny didn't want to play checkers, and after the Bible reading she went without being told to get ready for bed.

"Let me see your neck. And the bottoms of your feet," called Mrs. Logan.

Jenny came near for the inspection.

"Good. You're all clean."

Mrs. Logan smiled, but she did not reach out to touch the little girl.

Mr. Logan folded up the newspaper he had been reading.

"Kind of chilly tonight. Maybe Lady would like to stay in. What do you think?"

"Can she sleep in my room?" Jenny asked. Her face was hopeful, almost smiling.

"Can if she wants to."

"Come on, Lady. Come to bed."

Lady got up, wagging her tail. As Jenny opened the stair door, Mrs. Logan flipped on the hall light. "Leave the register open so the heat will come up." Then she leaned down and whispered in the little girl's ear, "But no eavesdropping."

Jenny got into bed. Lady sat down and let her front legs slide out slowly until she was lying down. The hall light poured in across the bottom of Jenny's bed, showing up the tufts of yarn in the quilt. Lady sighed. Jenny put her head down and stroked the dog's silky head.

"Stay here all night, Lady."

Somewhere between strokes, both Jenny and Lady fell asleep. When Mrs. Logan came up to bed, Jenny woke up and listened. Mrs. Logan stopped at Jenny's door for a moment, then went quietly away.

Jenny suddenly felt as if she wanted to cry.

4

THE REQUEST

The next few days were clear and warm. Jenny went to the mountain with Mr. Logan every time he made a trip. The day he mowed hay, she stayed with Mrs. Logan.

As she and the old woman weeded the garden after breakfast, Jenny could see Mr. Logan on the hill behind the barn. He was oiling his mowing machine. Sometimes he would be out of view behind the cutter bar and swathboard. Then he would stand up again, trying the action of the blade.

Jenny returned to her weeding.

"Is this a weed?" she asked.

Mrs. Logan leaned across a row of carrots, the knuckles of one hand sinking into the dirt as she did.

"Yes. And that sprig right beside it is too." Some hairs had escaped her braids and wisped around her face. She smiled at Jenny.

Jenny did not smile.

"You don't have to weed the whole garden," Mrs. Logan told her. "Just do your row of rhubarb, and then go do what you want."

"There's nothing else to do," Jenny said.

Mrs. Logan made no reply. When she kneeled in the rows of the garden, Mrs. Logan looked younger, Jenny thought. After a while Jenny spoke again.

"He wouldn't let me go cut hay with him."

"He thinks it isn't safe, I suppose."

"He didn't say why. He just said, 'Can't take you today.'" Jenny threw a weed on the pile.

Mrs. Logan looked up for a moment toward the place where her husband was working and smiled a quiet smile. Then she began weeding again, and without looking at Jenny, replied, "He doesn't always give his reason, but he generally has one."

After lunch, they picked elderberries. They washed the berries at the pump, Jenny working the handle mightily. Water gushed forth over the berries and Mrs. Logan's hands. Jenny liked the sparkle of the cold water in the sun.

"Enough, Jenny. We're done," Mrs. Logan said. The berries made a purple heap in the kettle.

Mrs. Logan said as she looked at the pump, "This old pump needs some paint. What do you say we paint it?"

That sounded interesting to Jenny. Mrs. Logan went to get the paint and two brushes. Jenny ate a few berries while she waited.

"What do you suppose Grandpa will say when he sees this?" Mrs. Logan said as they stood back admiring the gleaming red pump.

"Will he be mad?" Jenny's concern bordered on alarm.

"Oh, no. Not mad. He might say it was a waste of paint, though. I think it looks pretty. Matches the shutters on the house here. Well, it's done, anyway, isn't it?"

At supper, Mr. Logan made no comment about the pump. Nor did he say anything after supper. Jenny began to wonder if he had even seen it.

Finally, just before bedtime, as he was putting away the checkers, he said to his wife, "Eda, what did you paint the pump for?"

"It needed it."

"Did you use my shutter paint?"

"Yes, I did."

"Well, why didn't you paint the trough, too, while you were at it?" he asked, somewhat gruffly.

"I didn't want to waste the paint," she returned, folding up the crossword puzzle.

On Sunday, they dressed in their best clothes and drove over to the church. Mr. Logan wore his suit that was the color of oats, a white shirt, and a wide plaid tie. Mrs. Logan had on her navy blue dress with the white lace collar. She wore lipstick on Sundays and a small navy blue hat with a veil. Jenny looked down at her own clothes and wished she had a dress that was just for Sunday.

She didn't want to go to her Sunday school class, so she stayed with the Logans. Running her fingers along the scrollwork on the end of the pew, Jenny watched the preacher. He walked back and forth in front of the first pew, talking and carrying a large, floppy Bible. A fly meandered down the back of the seat in front of her. A breeze and pale sunlight came in through the open windows. Jenny swung her legs to keep awake.

Church began. Everyone stood up to sing "Praise God from Whom All Blessings Flow." Jenny did not sing but merely watched the others. Jacob, who picked up the milk, stood across the aisle in a blue suit. He looked so clean in church that Jenny was never really sure it was him. His wife sang loudly, closing her eyes often and clutching the songbook.

A big man with blond hair sang "I'm Just a Poor Wayfaring Stranger." His deep voice thrilled Jenny; the tune seemed lonely and beautiful. "I'm just a-going over Jordan; I'm just a-going over home." Long after he sat down, Jenny heard the music and repeated the words to herself.

The sermon was about not getting discouraged. Jenny did not listen well. She looked out the window at the tall grass in the meadow. Butterflies wafted up and down, their wings moving gracefully, almost sleepily.

"Now, Nehemiah had every reason to be discouraged," the preacher was saying.

At the name Nehemiah, Jenny came back to the sermon. She glanced at Mrs. Logan, who smiled knowingly at her.

"But he cared more about the work and the other people than he cared about himself. One of the best ways to meet up with discouragement is to care too much about yourself."

Soon everyone was standing, the whole church vibrating with "Rock of Ages." Mrs. Logan's strong alto surprised Jenny; the woman's voice seemed bigger than the woman.

"Good morning, Nicholas. Eda," said a thin woman behind them after the last *Amen*. "My, isn't this a pretty Sunday?"

"Very pretty," said Mrs. Logan. "And how have you been?"

"Much better, thanks. Good morning, Jenny. Did you eat all those blueberries I gave you?"

"We made jelly out of them," said Jenny, ducking her head.

"That's a good idea." She turned back to Mrs. Logan. "Say, Eda, I'm going into town in the morning. Anything you want me to pick up?"

"Well, I don't believe so, thanks, Marion. But I appreciate your asking."

"All right; call if you think of something."

Mrs. Logan and Jenny meandered toward the car, Mrs. Logan stopping to talk several times.

"Where's Grandpa?" Mrs. Logan asked when they finally reached the car. "He's usually out here waiting to go."

Soon he came, putting on his hat and getting the keys out of his pocket.

"Slow today, Nicholas," said Mrs. Logan.

"Yep."

As they came down over the hill to their house, Mr. Logan laughed a little chuckling laugh.

"Look there what we have, will you," he said and nodded toward the pasture.

"Oh, a calf!" cried Mrs. Logan, clapping her gloved hands. "Isn't it sweet? Slow down a bit, Nicholas!"

He stopped at the end of the driveway, and they all went up to the fence in their Sunday clothes to see the new baby.

"What a dandy," said Mr. Logan. "Wasn't Dolly busy while we were away?" He laughed.

Jenny looked wonderingly at the calf. It looked wet and wobbly. She did not think it was cute.

"He's sticky looking," she said.

The Logans laughed merrily.

"Tomorrow," said Mrs. Logan, "it'll look better."

And the calf did look better the next day. The white on it was a brilliant white, and the soft hair curled around its neck and stomach. When it tottered after its mother, it made a timid bleating sound.

"Like the calf better today?" Mr. Logan asked her.

"Yes."

"I'm glad you do because we're going to keep her. And it's your job to give her a name. What do you think of that?"

Jenny said nothing but stood looking through the fence at the cow and the calf.

"Take your time. Think of a good name," he told her.

After lunch, a car drove in. The woman who had sat behind them in church the day before got out carrying books and a bag of peaches.

Mrs. Logan stepped out on the porch, wiping her hands on her apron.

"Afternoon, Marion."

"Hello, Eda. Hello, Jenny."

"Was it hot in town?" Mrs. Logan asked.

"Not so very. I brought these peaches for you to try. I know they're a bit early, but I thought maybe we could open a few. If they're any good, I'll run back tomorrow and get us a couple bushels."

"Let's have a look at them."

"And here are the books Nicholas wanted from the library. I don't know why a woodsman like him wants books on forestry, but here they are." The neighbor lady held out the books.

Mrs. Logan smiled slightly, taking them. "Hard to say. Jenny, will you lay these books in by Grandpa's chair, please?"

Jenny took the books and went inside.

She paged through one book, the largest, with color pictures of leaves and bark. She knew the oak, birch, red maple, and silver maple leaves from having seen them in the woods.

As she stood looking at the book, she heard the women talking on the porch.

"What about Jenny? Is she staying?" Marion asked.

"We don't know yet. Sally and John Stebbs—over in Mileston, you know—are going to talk to the welfare people for us. I wish we'd hear something. Thursday is her last day."

"It would be bad if she had to leave. For her and you."

"It'll be sad, I'll tell you. Sometimes I just want to grab her up and hide her. Nicholas will be sick. He adores her."

Jenny heard no more. She felt her heart beating fast, and her face get hot. Clutching the books to her chest, she sat down in the rocking chair. For the first time in her life that she could remember, she wanted to stay where she was.

A long time later, Mrs. Logan came in.

"Reading those forestry books, are you?"

Jenny ran to her and clasped her about the waist, feeling the starched apron against her cheek.

A surprised Mrs. Logan bent down to draw Jenny close. She laid her cheek against Jenny's head.

An instant later Jenny broke free and ran out of the house. She felt happy and embarrassed and almost nervous. Before she stopped running, she had come to the upper pasture, where Benjamin grazed lazily. She stopped, panting, and leaned against the fence.

The old horse moved slowly, barely lifting his huge feet. Every now and then, he gave a great cough, and his sides bulged out amazingly, then sank back in.

Jenny gathered some purple clover from along the creek and threw it over the fence to Benjamin. He ate it eagerly. Then he moseyed nearer to her, perhaps expecting more clover. She backed up, a little afraid he would keep walking right through the fence. He was the biggest animal Jenny had ever seen.

She walked on up to the level place at the foot of the mountain where Mr. Logan was cutting up the logs he had brought out of the woods. The tractor was hooked up to the huge saw with a wide leather belt. The engine of the tractor turned the blade constantly. The blade made a fine, whirring hum when it wasn't cutting anything. When a log was put to it, it made a high, screaming noise, then a rattling sound, and then it settled into a steely buzz.

Jenny watched from a distance as Mr. Logan sawed the logs into sections. The chunks dropped in the sawdust, one after the other. Mr. Logan stopped to wipe his face with his handkerchief and then stuffed the red square back into his pocket. When he saw Jenny, he shut off the machinery.

"Hey, there! Come to help?"

"What can I do?" asked Jenny, jumping down the bank.

"Well, you can help stack the wood when I get it chopped."

Then they both heard a bell ringing from the house.

"The bell! The bell!" she cried.

"We're not late for supper, that's sure. We'd better go see what's the matter."

Down they went to the house, Jenny running and Mr. Logan and Lady coming behind. At the crest of the knoll above the house, Jenny stopped suddenly. Mrs. McAllister's car was in the driveway.

In the kitchen, Mrs. McAllister sat in the rocker. She had a warm and pleasant look. She smiled broadly as Jenny and the woodsman came in.

"My, my, Jenny! Look how tan you are. And such rosy cheeks!"

"Hello," said Jenny.

"This country air must be good for you. Hello, Mr. Logan." Her eyes met his with open friendliness.

"Good afternoon," he answered pleasantly.

"Have you been cutting wood again?" She turned to Jenny.

"I was just watching."

Mrs. McAllister laughed lightly. "Is that how you get such strong arms and legs? Just watching?"

"Sometimes I carry branches."

"I see. Think she might be a woodsman, Mr. Logan?"

"She already is one," he returned, smiling his amused smile.

"Do you like the woods, Jenny?" the woman asked.

"Yes."

"That's good," said Mrs. McAllister. "I'm glad to see you taking a liking to something."

"She has a good row of rhubarb in the garden, too, that she looks after," Mrs. Logan put in.

"You don't need to convince me that this is the place for Jenny. One look at her tells me that. But I'm afraid my superiors aren't so ready to see the light."

"Meaning Mr. Wright?" asked the old man.

"Well, yes. He and Miss Paterson, mostly. They went to the director after they were here. Miss Paterson could be convinced, I think. But Mr. Wright, well." She looked out the window and then back to the farmer. "Your age is a real problem down at the office, Mr. Logan. *I* know you can work about ninety percent of them into the ground. But that doesn't change the number on the paper. Do you know what I mean?"

"So what are you telling me?" he asked.

She sighed. "After Mrs. Stebbs talked to me, I went right back to the board and pleaded your case. I told them how Jenny's taking an interest in things and all. Of course, Mr. Wright had his say too. But the director is a very reasonable man; he's willing to listen. He doesn't make hasty decisions."

"And?" Mr. Logan's face was set. The lines around his eyes tightened.

"And all I could get was a six-months' trial period."

His face relaxed; he almost smiled. "Why, that's something, anyway. We've got a chance now, don't you think?"

"Slight. Slight. I'll do my utmost, I assure you. But a lot of people with more say than I have are not likely to change their minds."

"Why? Because I'm sixty-six?" he asked with a mixture of scorn and disbelief.

"I'll tell you the truth, Mr. Logan. But know first these are not my opinions. I think your keeping Jenny is a good arrangement. I thought so from the first. But Mr. Wright and Miss Paterson noticed your wood stove here and the small dairy herd and a few other things. And, well, they maintain that Jenny wouldn't get the best care here."

Mr. Logan leaned forward, putting his elbows on his knees, holding his cap in one hand, and turning it around with the other.

"I can't change my age. And I can't change my life. We live the way we live."

"I'm not saying you should change at all. *You're* not the ones who should change."

His eyes glistened, and he didn't look up. "So why don't you just take her now?"

"Because, maybe, just maybe, if we work it right, we can show them in six months' time that I've been right all along." She smiled hopefully at him.

"And if we don't? Then what? What about my poor little Jenny then?"

The clock ticked solemnly away above their heads. A tiny breeze lifted the edge of the curtain over the sink and fluttered the blossoms on the African violet on the sill.

Jenny stood silently by the door.

"It's a chance, I'll admit. But shouldn't we try, Mr. Logan?" Mrs. McAllister's voice was low.

He did not answer but stared ahead about three feet.

Mrs. Logan watched him. Lady sat up and put her ears forward, sensing something was wrong. Finally he said in a quiet, gruff voice: "I don't think we should take chances with a little girl's life. If we lose now, it's bad enough. But if we lose in six months, that would be six times worse. She'd be six times as settled, six times as at home here."

"You wouldn't be giving up, would you, Nicholas?" asked Mrs. Logan with a slight arch of the eyebrow.

He said nothing. The kitchen was silent except for the clock.

For Jenny, six months had no measure. It was an endless length of time, reaching past the scope of the worrisome future, past all bounds, pushing the dreaded leaving into some remote corner. She remembered only that he had said "my Jenny." She hesitated, leaning against the door behind her.

Then she moved forward and stepped up close to his chair. "I want to stay," she whispered to him.

He looked up at her for a moment and then leaned back in his chair. His skin had a wonderful smoothness for a man his age.

"Well, then," he said to Mrs. McAllister, "she stays."

That evening after supper, the Logans, Lady, and Jenny sat on the porch, the old people in wooden lawn chairs, Jenny beside Lady on the top step.

"Look at all those stars," said Mrs. Logan to no one in particular. "The Lord just sprinkled them out of heaven like sugar over a pie." Jenny looked up again to see the comparison.

Mr. Logan took out his watch, leaned over to get the light coming from the kitchen door. "About nine o'clock, it says here."

"Better get a bath, Jenny," Mrs. Logan said.

"Say, what about a name for the new calf? Did you think of a good one?" Mr. Logan inquired.

"Yes."

"Well, good. Let's hear it."

Jenny put her face against Lady's white neck and peeked up over her collar. She looked at Mr. Logan.

"I want to call her Eda."

"Eda! Now if that's not a good name, I don't know one!" laughed Mr. Logan.

Mrs. Logan put down her crocheting and laughed with her husband. "See that you don't get us mixed up," she warned him, giggling in her way.

"Oh no," he answered, "the calf can't crochet."

5

THE LAMP
AND THE BOX

Summer vacation ended. School began. Jenny enrolled in the third grade in the school at the crossroads. Only knowing Teresa and Lynn Stebbs, she either played with them at recess or she stayed by herself at first. After a few weeks she made friends with Carrie Meyer in her own grade, and they sat together on the bus.

Mornings were getting colder, the days shorter. By Carrie's house the maple trees had started to turn a brilliant orange. Every day Jenny studied the trees, amazed at how fast the orange spread through the limbs. Dotted across the mountains, other early trees turned red and gold, standing out sharply against the greens and browns of late summer.

Mrs. Logan cut up dresses that her daughter sent from Texas to make new outfits for Jenny. Jenny always wondered how anything she would like could come out of box of hand-me-downs; but somehow the new dress was always pretty and it always fit.

Mrs. Logan even made her a burgundy dress with lace cuffs that was just for Sunday. Sometimes Jenny went to the closet on a weekday just to look at it. Now on Sunday mornings, she put on her Sunday dress, the same as Mrs. Logan did.

One afternoon Jenny and Mrs. Logan went to the attic to get books to read after supper. Narrow wooden steps rose up into a dusty darkness. Mrs. Logan carried a flashlight, but its beam could not reach the corners. Jenny drew back.

"Wait and I'll light the lamp," said Mrs. Logan. She climbed to the top without Jenny. From below Jenny heard her scrape a match, and then she saw Mrs. Logan in the light of its little flame.

The kerosene lamp flickered into a steady glow. Its clean light opened up the darkness all around.

"Wow, that makes a big light, doesn't it?" said Jenny.

"It's an Aladdin lamp. There. Now we can see what we're doing."

Jenny came up the steps to Mrs. Logan. In the attic the air seemed drier. The cobwebs in the rafters made Jenny want to keep her head down.

Mrs. Logan opened a pine chest, the hinges squeaking softly.

"Look here, Jenny. This is a quilt my mother made."

Jenny looked. Underneath the quilt was a dress.

"That was one of my mother's Sunday dresses."

"How old is it?" Jenny asked.

"About seventy-five years, I guess. And look, here's a shawl." She wrapped it around Jenny with a wink. "Now you're a lady from the 1880s."

Jenny giggled. "Can I wear the dress?"

"When you are big enough to fit into it."

"Here are the books," said Mrs. Logan, opening a crate.

"Here's *Heidi*. And here's *Lassie, Come Home*." She continued to sort through the books.

"Grandma," said Jenny.

"Yes, honey?" answered Mrs. Logan without looking up from her sorting.

"Whose books are these?"

"They belonged to my children many years ago."

"So that's their crate of stuff?"

Mrs. Logan glanced up, puzzled. "One of the many."

"I want to keep something in the attic too."

"Oh," laughed the old lady, "I see. Well, what do you want to keep up here?"

"I don't know. But I want to put something up here so in a hundred years someone will say 'I wonder whose stuff this is.' And then they will open the box and all my things will be old."

"All right. That's a good idea, Jenny. Let's see if any of these trunks are empty."

Most of the trunks and boxes were full, but at last they found a big wooden box with only locks and bolts in it. Mrs. Logan put the metal pieces in an old tea can.

"Now," she said, "all we need is something of yours to put in the box. What shall it be?"

Jenny sat thinking.

"I use everything I have."

"How about that yellow skirt you don't like to wear?"

"Okay!" Then she stopped smiling. "But that's only one thing."

"True. But I've been filling up this attic for forty years. I don't expect we'll get this big box filled up any too soon, do you?"

"I guess not."

"Now go get that skirt while I sort through the rest of these books."

The days became crisper, clearer. Many days a steady wind came down off the mountain, taking with it some leaves. Jenny liked to wander by the creek on such days. Sometimes, when the sun was strong and warm, she put her feet in the icy water. Dried stalks leaned off the bank and bobbed in the wind. All around her the world said good-bye to summer and looked toward the coming cold.

Mr. Logan built a new stall in the barn for Benjamin on the south side. The wind, he had explained, would not be as fierce there, and the old horse would have a more comfortable winter. If he were working in the barn when Jenny came from school, Jenny would help him, handing him nails or carrying boards.

"Can we build a special place for Eda?" she asked him one afternoon.

"The other cows might be jealous, mightn't they?" he asked over his shoulder.

"Cows don't get jealous," Jenny replied, looking at him with a knowledgeable smile.

"These do. Millie especially. She thinks she's the head cow around here," he said.

Jenny giggled. "Our cows are better than anyone else's."

"Why is that?"

"They have more character."

She stressed the word *character* by drawing it out and nodding her head as she said it. "Everything on this farm has character."

"Who says?" he asked with a short laugh.

"Grandma."

"Well, she ought to know," he said.

"She says nobody gets anywhere without it."

"No place worth going, I guess. I'm out of nails, Miss Jenny Wren."

She brought more nails and changed the topic.

"Do you have Grandma's surprise done yet?"

"Nope."

"When will it be done?"

"Christmas."

"Christmas! That's a long time yet."

"To you, maybe. But I've got a lot to do still. You're doing a good job keeping the secret, Jenny. I'm proud of you."

"I didn't even tell Carrie."

"That's the stuff." He winked at her.

"Where's Lady?" she asked, changing to yet another topic.

"In the house."

"Did she go with you to cut wood?"

"Yep. And now she's all tired out."

"Why?" asked Jenny.

"Well, she's getting kind of old for all that travel."

"How old is she?"

"In dog years, I'd say she's about seventy."

"She's older than you!"

"That's pretty old, you think, I suppose."

She gave no answer but laughed and ran out the side bottom door of the barn and into the pasture. The day was so beautiful that she wanted to run up the hill and try to absorb it somehow.

After supper and homework, Mr. Logan took out a book he had been reading and called Jenny over. She sat on the floor by the stove, her arm around Lady's neck and her knees under her chin.

"I'm going to tell you what I've read," he told her, "about how the trees take turns owning the forest, as you call it.

"Now, let's say we let this pasture out here go. We won't plow it or mow it or anything. We just let it stand. After a few years, seeds—carried by birds and animals and wind—start to come up. Little trees, that would normally get plowed under or mowed off, get a chance to grow.

"Now the trees that can take strong sunlight, like birches, grow up fast. But they only live a little while. Their branches, though, block out the bright sun, so the weeds die off and trees that like shade have a chance to grow. Trees like the red oaks and maples."

"Why don't the birches keep making little birches come up like they do in the yard?" asked Jenny.

"They do. But the big birches make too much shade for them and they don't get big.

"All the field animals—little field mice and that kind, you know, leave then because a forest has begun. Forest birds and animals come. Deer come and thrushes and like that.

"After a long time the red oaks and maples get old and die off. But all that time, the leaves that fall every year have been making a rich soil in the forest. You know how it is up on the mountain."

He looked at her, and she nodded.

"Then the hemlocks and that kind of tree come up. They like the shade and the rich soil and they grow very slowly. So as an oak or a maple falls, a young pine rises slowly to take its place. You see?"

"Yes," said Jenny after a moment. "How long does all that take?"

"A couple hundred years or more."

Jenny said no more, her attention beginning to wander.

"I'm glad you're out of questions," he said, putting aside the book, "because that's about all I know to tell you."

"You know everything."

"No," he laughed. "But you can usually find what you want to know in a book."

"Can we read *Heidi* now, Grandma?" said Jenny, turning to Mrs. Logan, who was doing a puzzle.

"One chapter, then. Get the book."

6

THE OLD HORSE

The next morning the ground was thick with frost. Everywhere the white veil lay, glistening in the early sun.

"Ice on the water bucket this morning," Mr. Logan told his wife at breakfast.

"Fall's here," she said, a little sadly. "Did the frost get my dahlias?"

"Afraid so. Froze things even under the trees last night."

"Well, we'd better pull in for winter soon."

Jenny listened to their conversation. There was something comfortable about it, like coming inside from the dark.

"I brought Benjamin down from the pasture this morning. He'll be better off in the barn from now on."

"Poor old Ben," was all Mrs. Logan answered.

After school, Jenny went to the barn to see the horse in his new stall. The afternoon sun slanted through the windows and made a hazy light in the stanchions.

The huge horse stood in his sturdy stall, chewing slowly on fresh hay. With his coat brushed and his mane and tail untangled, he looked almost friendly. Jenny stepped carefully up to the side slats. Benjamin turned his head to look at her. She could smell his breath; it smelled of hay and clover. He watched her a moment, then turned back to his hay, jerking a mouthful free from the rack with a twist of his head.

Jenny backed away from the stall and ran outside. She scanned the bank for a fallen apple that would be big enough for Benjamin. Just as she found one, Mr. Logan came up behind her.

"Are you going to eat that?" he asked.

"No. It's for Benjamin."

"I thought so. Don't give him but one a day, you hear?"

She nodded.

"And be sure you hold your hand out flat—like this—or he might get your fingers by mistake."

Her eyes opened wide.

"Just do what I tell you," he said, breaking into a smile, "and you'll be all right."

Jenny went back inside. Benjamin's hooves were the largest she had ever seen. But he stood so still that his size did not frighten her as much as it had before.

Slowly she reached her hand through the slats, holding the apple in her flat palm. Benjamin stretched his neck forward and sniffed the fruit. Suddenly he bit the apple in half. Jenny jumped back, dropping the other half. Benjamin nibbled it up from the straw.

And then she was immediately sorry. Poor Benjamin wouldn't have hurt her. When he lifted his head to her again, she put out her hand and stroked his nose. He blinked slowly.

"You're a pretty nice horse," she told him.

Benjamin swung his head around to bite a fly on his side. Then he looked at Jenny again, flaring his nostrils, sniffing.

"I can give you only one apple today," she said apologetically. "Wait 'til tomorrow."

The old horse seemed to understand because he sighed wearily and then jerked another mouthful of hay from the rack. Once in a while a fly would light on him. A quiver of a shoulder or a swish of a tail usually sent the pest winging away.

"Pretty soon these flies will freeze up, Benjamin," she told him. "Winter's coming. And you have this warm place to be."

He chewed on noisily.

Jenny leaned against the slats. The smell of hay and wood and horse mixed together. She liked the smell.

Then Mr. Logan came in. Jenny asked him, "Did you ever ride Benjamin?"

"No. He's a plow horse, not a pleasure horse."

"Could you ride him?"

"I suppose if I had to."

Jenny said nothing more. She noticed how Benjamin's coat looked a little fuzzy in the sunlight.

"Do you want to ride him?" Mr. Logan asked.

A thrill of terror went through Jenny. She felt like running and laughing all at once.

"No." The quietness of her answer belied the pounding in her chest.

"Sure?" Mr. Logan looked down at her with the little smile he always had when he knew more than he was letting on to know.

"He's too big," she said.

Mr. Logan opened the stall and walked in. He patted the horse's neck and drew his fingers through the mane.

"You wouldn't hurt our little Jenny, would you?" he asked the horse.

Jenny hung back, wanting to go in the stall but fearing to.

"Come on in, Jenny." His voice compelled her. "Ben won't hurt you. And I'll be right here."

She didn't move.

"Jenny."

She stepped half sideways to the opening, looking steadily at the old man.

"Come on," he said.

She went inside the stall but not near the horse. Benjamin turned his head to look at her. He seemed like a wall or a mountain. She could hear his breathing.

"Jenny's come to see you, Ben. What do you think of that?"

Benjamin nosed Mr. Logan's shirt pocket.

"Feel how soft his nose is."

Jenny still hesitated. Mr. Logan waited. At length, she came forward and touched the animal's nose.

"He's so big," she said in a whisper.

"That's so. But you needn't be afraid of him. Treat him right and he'll treat you right."

"How?" She could hardly hear over the pounding of her heart.

"Well, don't walk behind him fast or brush his hair the wrong way or give him an apple with your fingers curled up. Now, shall I put you up?"

Benjamin chewed a mouthful of hay and shifted his weight. Behind her, Jenny felt the rough boards of the stall. Mr. Logan held the halter strap loosely, looking from Jenny to Benjamin and back to Jenny.

A long time passed. Then Jenny nodded, not looking at Mr. Logan.

Before she could muster her courage, the old man had scooped her up and onto the horse's back. She seemed to be awfully high up, and the horse's back was so wide that she felt the muscles in her legs stretch.

She took hold of the dark mane in both hands, sitting somewhat stiffly in controlled fear. Benjamin took a step back, and Jenny felt as if the earth had moved and surely she would fall. She felt numb and dizzy and slightly sick.

"All right?" Mr. Logan asked from beside her and below.

Jenny Wren

She nodded. She sat absolutely still until the new perspective on everything began to seem normal. Benjamin went on chewing and looking around, apparently unconcerned that he was being sat upon. In a little while Jenny believed that she liked the seat.

"Want to stay there while I get the cows?" Mr. Logan asked.

Jenny did not want to miss seeing the cows come over the hill.

"Can I sit here during milking?"

"If you want."

"Then I'll get down now."

When he lifted her down to the deep straw, her legs were wobbly. She hoped Mr. Logan didn't notice.

"Lady and I will get the cows." She left the stall and called for the dog.

Every evening after that, Jenny perched on Benjamin and watched the milking go on from the new vantage point. When the horse shifted his weight, Jenny rode with him. After a while she began to wish she could ride in the open field.

She would think about being astride a silky horse, gliding through the meadows, winning races, taking prizes at horse shows. Then Mr. Logan would call her, and she would slide off old Benjamin and run ahead of Mr. Logan and Lady to the house.

One afternoon, Jenny came home from school full of news.

"Guess what happened at school today?" she said, bursting into the kitchen where Mrs. Logan was rolling out pie dough.

"What?" Mrs. Logan turned from the counter and wiped her hands on a dish towel, listening.

"I told everybody how trees take turns owning the forest. I knew and no one else did."

"Well, tell me all the details," the lady said.

"See, Mrs. Carson was talking about how seeds grow and about all the things that come from seeds. Then she asked us where pine tree seeds came from."

"And?"

"And I said that they came on the little pieces of the pine cone and that pine trees don't grow very well in bright light."

Jenny was smiling broadly.

"And then?" Mrs. Logan's eyes were bright with interest.

"Then she asked me how they did grow."

"What did you say?"

"I told her all that stuff Grandpa told me from the books."

"Well, honey, I'm just real proud of you. You should tell Grandpa."

"Where is he?"

"Out at the barn, I guess."

Jenny ran out. The fall air was clear and warm. The colors of the leaves were at their peak; the mountain rose up a blaze of orange and gold behind the farmhouse and the barn. The shorn hayfields were the color of toast, and here and there swallows dipped and soared above them.

She found Mr. Logan standing between the barn and the creek. She watched him from the back barn door for a minute. He wasn't working at anything. He was just standing there in his overalls and workshirt, gazing at the stubble in the fields.

Quietly she came up behind him.

"Hi," she said.

"Well, it's Jenny Wren." He turned half around to see her, smiled, but did not uncross his arms.

"What are you doing?" she asked him.

"Looking."

Jenny turned her gaze to follow his. After a moment she spoke again.

"What are you looking at?"

"At this fine farm. What are you looking at?"

"You."

He laughed his chuckling laugh. Jenny wanted to tell him about her day at school, but somehow she couldn't think of how to bring it up.

"One day soon here, I'll have to be bringing the cows in for winter."

Jenny said nothing. It was very comfortable standing in the pasture in the afternoon sun with this big man. Lady came out of the shadow of the stone wall, walked up to Jenny, and volunteered to be petted. The little girl stroked the dog's head.

"Shall we go for the cows?" she asked.

"Not just yet. I'll do the milking tonight. I want you to help Grandma with supper. She's been canning all day, and she's pretty tired."

"Okay. Shall I come out to feed Eda?"

"Well, she might miss you, mightn't she? You better come and feed Eda. But see if Grandma needs you first."

Jenny strolled to the house. She stopped to pump the pump handle a few times. Then she studied the ants at the edge of the flowerbed. At last she went inside.

"Grandpa says you need help in here."

"He did?" Mrs. Logan glanced out the window above the sink.

"Well, you can set the table as always."

Jenny opened the silverware drawer and pulled out the knives and forks.

"Did you tell him about school?" Mrs. Logan asked.

"No." Jenny laid the silverware on the table.

"Was he busy?"

"No. He was looking."

Mrs. Logan put back the curtain and leaned across the sink to look out the window again.

"What was he looking at?"

"This fine farm."

Jenny put the blue and white plates down, turning them carefully so the birds and the trees would be right side up.

Mrs. Logan could see the cows coming in a line toward the barn. The setting sun laid a fine gold on the hills.

Jenny stood by the table. "What else?"

Mrs. Logan let the curtain fall back into place.

"Well, you could stir the soup while I check on the pie."

Later Jenny returned to the barn to feed Eda. The milking was nearly done.

"Did you think I wasn't coming?" she asked Eda.

To Jenny the barn seemed quiet tonight. She measured the calf feed and poured it into the box in Eda's stall. The calf was just learning to eat grain and so she made a funny, snuffling racket when she ate. Jenny filled a bucket with water and carried it in to the calf. The heifer slurped it noisily. Jenny tried to hold the bucket still. Finally it was empty.

"That's all, Eda. You sure are a hungry calf." She patted the animal's shoulder and then stood back to admire the size of her charge. "You're getting to be a big girl."

The calf blinked her huge brown eyes in response. The long eyelashes never failed to amaze Jenny.

She stopped by Benjamin's stall. He stood silently with his head down.

"Hey, Benjamin. Did you miss me? We didn't go to the races tonight, did we?" She giggled.

She ran out to see if there were any apples left on the bank. There were a few. She selected the biggest one.

"Come on to supper," Mr. Logan said, hanging up the pail.

"I have to give Benjamin an apple first."

"No, come now, Jenny."

She looked at him questioningly but dropped the apple without comment.

When they entered the kitchen, Mrs. Logan looked at her husband with a little arch in her eyebrow. He gave no sign that he noticed.

"Do you have any schoolwork tonight?" he asked Jenny during supper.

"No. I got it done at school."

Mrs. Logan picked up the topic. "Seems Jenny was pretty smart in class today."

"Oh?" Mr. Logan cocked his head and gave Jenny that half-sly smile he had.

"Told everyone how trees take turns owning the forest," Mrs. Logan said.

"That right?" He smiled fully.

"Yes," Jenny said, finally getting to what she wanted to talk about. "I told them how a field left to itself will become a woods. And how pine trees come up, and everything."

"Well, that's the stuff." He winked at her.

"What did Mrs. Carson say?" Mrs. Logan asked.

"She said I could do a bulletin board about it if I wanted to."

"Wonderful! Will you do one?"

"Yes, I think I will."

Mrs. Logan reached out and patted Jenny's hand.

"Say," the lady said to her husband, "there was an antique dealer here today."

"Oh?"

"You were buzzing logs. I told him we didn't have anything to sell."

He smiled and nodded to his wife.

"I think we should put out a sign—'No Antiques for Sale,'" she said.

"Unless you want to sell me," he said. And she laughed.

After the evening tasks, Mrs. Logan read the last of *Heidi* aloud. They all agreed that it had been a good book.

Jenny sat in Mr. Logan's lap all the while.

He rocked steadily back and forth and patted her knee on every rock back.

After several minutes he said, "I think Benjamin might be sick."

Jenny pushed away from his shoulder to look him in the face.

"How sick? Sick with what?"

"I don't know." The answer was for both questions.

"When did you notice?" Mrs. Logan asked.

"This morning."

There was silence all around.

"He'll get better, won't he?" Jenny stared at him intently.

"He might."

She sank back against his shoulder.

Jenny Wren

"Anyway," he continued, "no apples or rides for a while."

Mr. Logan read from the Psalms later. Jenny liked the way the words sounded together.

Like as a father pitieth his
children, so the Lord pitieth
them that fear him.
For he knoweth our frame;
he remembereth that we are dust.
As for man, his days are as
grass; as a flower of the field,
so he flourisheth.
For the wind passeth over
it, and it is gone; and the
place thereof shall know it
no more.
But the mercy of the Lord
is from everlasting to
everlasting upon those who fear
him, and his righteousness
unto children's children.

Jenny thought of the fields and of the wind along the creek. It was pleasant to think of the fields and listen to the old words.

The old people prayed. Jenny opened her eyes and watched their faces. It was rather strange, she thought, as if they were away from her. She waited for them to pray for Benjamin. And when they did not, she wished she knew how to pray.

That night when Jenny got into bed, she put her arms out to Mrs. Logan. The old lady bent down and pulled her close. Jenny hung on so tightly that Mrs. Logan sat down on the bed and pulled her up to herself. She continued to sit there until Jenny fell asleep in her arms.

7

THE FIRST SNOW

Nothing much was said about Benjamin for the next two days. He didn't look any different to Jenny. Although he didn't eat constantly as he once had, he still stood in his stall, dozing or watching the cows. Jenny was satisfied.

The weather turned solidly cold, frosts settling with a clean, hard look on the fields and hills. A little lace of frost hung in the corners of Jenny's bedroom windows each morning. She found she had to stand over the register several minutes before she had the courage to get dressed.

Mrs. Logan lined the cellar shelves with canned tomatoes, peaches, beans, and pickles. Mr. Logan had dug the potatoes out of the garden, and Jenny had helped unload them into the cellar bin. On Saturday, while he put the storm windows on the house, Jenny and Mrs. Logan put away summer clothes and got out winter ones.

"Jenny, I don't think these dungarees will fit you another summer. Why don't you put them in your box in the attic?"

Jenny laid them on the bed to take to the attic later. She watched as Mrs. Logan hung her summer things in the back of the closet. It occurred to Jenny that she didn't have many winter clothes.

"How long will winter be here?" she asked.

"A good long time," said Mrs. Logan. Jenny could not tell whether the woman was sad or glad about that.

"Will there be lots of snow?"

"Plenty. And then some."

Jenny's wool skirts and sweaters now hung in a neat row in the front of the closet.

"Now, my dear, you come with me. I have something to show you," Mrs. Logan said.

She followed the lady into the Logans' bedroom. Mrs. Logan opened her own closet door.

"I have a few things for you to try on," she was saying as she laid dresses, blouses, skirts, and finally a coat on the bed.

"Did your daughter send all these things?" Jenny asked, dazedly. It was as if someone had cleaned off a department store rack.

"Yes. And I've taken everything in. Let's see how they fit."

Everything fit as if it had been bought for her. The last outfit she put on was a burgundy corduroy skirt and vest with a burgundy print shirt. There was a hanky out of the shirt material in the pocket of the vest. She gazed at herself in Mrs. Logan's big mirror. She could only smile and smile.

"That looks pretty, Jenny; don't you think?"

She nodded, not taking her eyes away from the mirror.

"Here. Try on the coat."

Jenny turned to put her arm in the sleeve. She thought of something that made her stop.

"Is this brand new?"

"It sure is. I hope it fits."

"Is this from your daughter, too?"

"Um-hmn," Mrs. Logan said through the pins she held in her mouth. "It's a little long. We'll fix that."

When the new clothes hung in Jenny's closet, the bar was full. One more hanger would have crowded things.

"Which daughter sent the clothes?" asked Jenny, looking at the photograph of the Logan family.

"This one," said Mrs. Logan, pointing to a pigtailed girl who dangled her legs over the edge of the porch.

Jenny glanced from the picture to Mrs. Logan and back to the picture.

"She looks like you."

"A little."

"I wish I did."

"You'd look pretty funny with gray hair." Mrs. Logan regarded the serious face turned up to her, then said, "Let's see if I can put your hair up like mine, shall we?"

Jenny sat at Mrs. Logan's dresser watching in the mirror as her hair was braided and pulled across the top of her head.

Then she looked down at the perfume and jewelry, the safety pins, the rubber bands, and the combs on the dresser. The dresser itself was a beautifully glossy wood with an unusual grain.

"What kind of wood is this?" Jenny asked.

Mrs. Logan did not look away from the braid she was pinning. "Curly maple. Grandpa made this dresser for me a long time ago. He said he'd make a frame for my mirror to match, but I think maybe he forgot."

Jenny remembered the wood she had seen Mr. Logan cutting on the barn floor one rainy day and kept silent.

"There," said the lady. "What do you think?"

They both looked at Jenny in the mirror.

Thick brown braids crisscrossed on the top of her head and framed her face, making it look round and smooth.

"It's nice," Jenny said.

"Looks too old on you, I think," said Mrs. Logan, straightening up.

"I wish I was as pretty as you," Jenny said.

Mrs. Logan blushed a little, her blue eyes getting a sparkle brighter than normal.

"You are prettier than I am, right now."

Jenny did not think so, but said nothing.

Mrs. Logan went on. "I'm an old lady. And here you are, full of color."

That wasn't what Jenny had meant by *pretty,* but she couldn't think how to explain what she did mean.

"If we were in a picture together, I would want people to think I was yours."

Mrs. Logan looked at the girl thoughtfully and tapped her chin with her finger as she did when she was considering something.

Jenny turned from the mirror image to the real face of Mrs. Logan. She studied the lines around her eyes and her gray braids. All at once the little girl felt lonely.

"I don't want Benjamin to die," she said, getting up from the dresser.

"Well, I don't either. But Jenny, nobody and nothing lives forever." She waited for Jenny to speak. When she didn't, the woman continued. "Benjamin has had a good, long life."

"I don't want anything to change!" Jenny's voice rang out in the quiet room.

"Jenny, listen—"

"No! He won't die. And we will go on doing chores and everything will be the same." Her eyes flashed at Mrs. Logan who still stood before the mirror. There was a pause. The old lady seemed to be debating with herself.

Finally she said calmly, evenly. "Only our Lord Jesus is the same yesterday, today, and forever."

"That's not what I mean."

Jenny's temper was surging underneath her level words.

Again the woman thought carefully before she spoke, looking steadily at the girl.

"The seasons change. The trees—" she began.

"But they come back! That's not what I'm talking about!" Jenny's voice was getting away from her.

Mrs. Logan did not look away from Jenny. "God never changes, Jenny. He is always there."

The child backed out of the bedroom. She had wanted Mrs. Logan to tell her that Benjamin would not die. "Say Benjamin won't die!"

"I can't." Mrs. Logan's voice was low and she put out her arms to Jenny. The little girl fled down the stairs.

"Jenny!" called Mrs. Logan. But Jenny had already run out toward the garden. She ran at an angle through the orchard until she was sure that she could not be seen from the bedroom window. She did not go back to the house all afternoon. But she did not go back to the barn either.

Supper was quiet. Jenny had spent her temper throwing rotting apples at the fence row. She felt tired. She was afraid Mrs. Logan would say something to Mr. Logan about the argument, but she did not.

Later Mrs. Logan read from the Bible as usual. But tonight it was not a story about a particular person or from one of the Psalms.

> Let your conversation be without covetousness; and be content with such things as ye have: for he hath said, I will never leave thee, nor forsake thee.

So that we may boldly say, The Lord is my helper, and I will not fear what man shall do unto me.

Remember them who have the rule over you, who have spoken unto you the word of God: whose faith follow, considering the end of their conversation.

Jesus Christ, the same yesterday, and to day, and for ever.

The woman closed the Bible and looked at Jenny. "If you believe that, Jenny, you'll never be alone." Jenny stared back. When Mr. Logan prayed, he prayed that Jenny would be happy and that she would understand that Jesus loved her enough to die for her.

She did not wait to be told it was bedtime.

The next day she sat in church looking at the lace cuffs on her Sunday dress. The toes of her shoes just reached the plank floorboards and sometimes when she wasn't thinking about holding her feet still, one or the other shoe would slip forward, and her leg would slip out before she could stop it.

Then she would glance up at Mrs. Logan to see if she noticed. Mrs. Logan never seemed to notice.

The sun came through the stained glass windows, pouring colors across the dark pews. Jenny could see bits of dust swirling in the beams of light, and it reminded her of being in the woods where the great shafts of light slanted down through the trees.

Soon everyone was up singing "Lord, I'm Coming Home." Jacob was there, and Marion, and Mrs. Carson. Jenny watched their faces but did not join in the singing. All she wanted was to be done with church and get home for the chicken dinner she knew would be there.

Mrs. Logan invited Marion Meyer and her husband Ralph for dinner. Then she said to Jenny, "Why don't you see if Carrie wants to come along to dinner? Her Grandma and Grandpa are coming, so they can take her home."

There was a full kitchen that Sunday. Lady tried to make herself known amid the hubbub but at last retreated to the solitude of the back porch.

Mr. Meyer in the rocker and Mr. Logan in the desk chair discussed the weather, the crops, the sermon, and the taxes. The ladies talked about the weather, the canning, the sermon, and the dinner. Jenny and Carrie wandered into the living room where a fire blazed in the fireplace to play until dinner. They decided on Chinese checkers.

"How come you don't come in our Sunday school class?" Carrie asked.

Jenny shrugged.

"Why don't you though?"

"I don't want to." She fished out the white marbles for Carrie.

"Are you related to the Logans?"

"No. I just stay here."

"I don't know if I'd like to live with my Grandma and Grandpa or not."

"Why?" Jenny put the red marbles on her side of the board without looking up.

"Old people are so . . . old," Carrie said.

"The Logans aren't old."

"They're as old as Grandma and Grandpa, I'll bet."

"It's your turn," Jenny said.

Mrs. Logan finally called everyone to the dining room.

At dinner the subject of Benjamin came up.

"I believe I'll catch Dr. Krieger tomorrow. Alan said the vet would be out to his place in the morning," Mr. Logan told Mr. Meyer.

"How old is that horse anyway?"

"Eighteen," Mr. Logan replied, with a note of pride, Jenny noticed.

"Old enough for a horse, I guess," the other man said.

The conversation went on to the Clarks' horses on the next farm and then on to something else, but Jenny quit listening.

Late that afternoon Mrs. Logan came out to the barn. Her coming made it seem like a special occasion, Jenny thought.

In the calf pen she told Eda, "Be good. Be good. Grandma's here to see you."

When Mrs. Logan came to the stall door, Jenny stood looking at the calf, wanting Mrs. Logan to say something. She was truly shocked when Mrs. Logan stepped down into the straw.

"What a fine calf," she was saying. She let the calf lick her hand and bump against her. Jenny watched in wonderment. "Isn't she a pretty one though. Look at those eyelashes!"

Jenny admired her calf anew.

Mrs. Logan left the calf pen and went to Benjamin's stall. She did not stand outside and reach through the slats. Rather she opened the gate, as one who had long been familiar with barns and horses.

"Well, Old Ben," Jenny heard her say. "What's got you so low?"

The horse raised his head to her, and she took his muzzle between her hands.

"There's a lot of plowed ground behind, isn't there?"

He gave his mane a little toss.

"And we don't forget it, Nicholas and I."

She stayed a while longer, then gave the huge animal a pat and left the stall.

Jenny and Mrs. Logan waited for Mr. Logan to finish milking.

"Better get along, I guess, or we'll be late for church," the old farmer said.

He closed the great barn door and then held out his arm to his wife. She linked her arm in his, and they started for the house. They walked very close together. Jenny and Lady followed them slowly.

The old couple said nothing as they walked. But Jenny knew if she spoke it would be an interruption.

The next morning there was a skiff of snow on the ground when Jenny left for school. She left reluctantly, wanting to be there when the veterinarian came, to hear what he would say.

She passed a weary day in school. In the middle of the afternoon, it began to snow again. The schoolroom bustled and rustled with the contained excitement.

"Maybe we can sled after school," Carrie whispered.

"Maybe," Jenny said.

At last the bell rang. A cheer went up, and there was much scuffling and shifting. The buses were waiting in the flying snow, their windshield wipers slapping and white exhaust churning out of the tailpipes.

"Look how much has stayed already," Carrie exclaimed. "Boy, it must be two inches."

Jenny gazed out the bus window distractedly. The bus was taking so long to get home tonight, she thought. Mr. Logan was waiting at the mailbox for the bus.

"Evening, Foster," he said to the driver. "Slippery, is it?"

"Not too bad. How's Eda?"

"Real good. How's Mary?"

"Pretty good. You folks should come down and visit."

"You're right. You're right. Thought I'd better come get my little girl here. She didn't wear any boots today."

"Well, here she is."

Mr. Logan picked Jenny up from the stairwell of the bus and stepped back.

"Thanks, Foster."

"You're more than welcome, Nicholas."

Mr. Logan carried Jenny toward the house. Lady joined them about halfway up. When he set Jenny down on the steps of the porch, she finally asked him the question.

"How's Benjamin?"

Mr. Logan looked at her. She felt the flakes hitting her cheek.

"He's gone, Jenny."

"No!" Her eyes grew wide. "I don't believe you!"

She ran through the snow, stumbling once, more because of her haste than because of the snow. She struggled with the heavy barn door.

It was dim in the barn, but she could see all the cows turn to look at her. Eda bawled from her pen.

Jenny walked up to Benjamin's stall and looked through the slats. It was empty.

8

THE NIGHT AWAY

Jenny's leather loafers sat drying on the enamel stove shelf. The kitchen was warm with the dry heat of a wood fire. Jenny sat at the desk, holding a book, but not reading it. It was nearly eight o'clock.

"Jenny," Mrs. Logan said. The girl did not look around. "Shall I make you something to eat? You didn't eat much supper."

"No, thank you." Her voice was low, empty.

Mrs. Logan looked at her husband, who was saddle-soaping his work shoes in front of the stove. When he finished, he took Jenny's shoes down to see if they were dry.

"Horses die," he said, finally. He began to rub saddle soap into one of her loafers. "And there's the end of it. I feel bad about Benjamin, too, Jenny. So does Grandma. We had him a long time. If I could change things back for you I would, Jenny Wren. But dying is a part of living. That's how it is."

Jenny's eyes stung, and her cheeks felt hot. She thought about getting ready for bed, but the whole effort seemed useless. People ought to just sit in chairs or hang from pegs on the wall all night, she thought. She continued to stare at her book.

After a while, Mrs. Logan came over and began to stroke Jenny's hair. Ducking her head, Jenny pulled away, not angrily, but with a weary feeling that made her want to cry.

When she finally got ready for bed, she went straight to the stair door. She did not go up to Mr. Logan for a kiss or wait for Mrs. Logan to get up and come with her. And when she saw Lady standing at the stair door wagging her tail, she frowned.

"Stay here," she told the dog. "Just stay down here."

"Oh, poor Lady," Mrs. Logan said.

Jenny hardened her heart, lest she pity the dog. "I don't want her in my room."

"You don't have to then. But Lady doesn't know what's the matter. She'll think she's done something wrong."

Jenny looked sullenly at Lady. She suddenly despised the gray hairs around the muzzle and the stiff way she sat down.

"I don't want her."

Mr. Logan studied the child from his rocker.

"Benjamin," he said, "was sick. Lady is not so old—and she is not sick."

Jenny's gaze shot up to his.

"I know what you think," he said. "You think that Lady is old, and I am, and Grandma is."

Jenny glared at him.

"You don't know what I think!"

"Don't I?"

Jenny whipped open the door.

"Just a minute." His voice was firm, and she hesitated.

"Jenny."

She let go of the door knob and looked at him.

"Come over here."

She went far enough to be counted obedient, but not so far that he would be able to touch her.

"I'm going to tell you this, and I want you to hear me."

Jenny could hear the fire snap in the stove.

"I won't lie to you. I am older than the other people you've stayed with. And I might die, though I don't expect to any time soon. But, Jenny, anyone might die. A man thirty years old can die as quick as I can. No one has any guarantees. Things never stay exactly the same all the time."

Jenny stared at the crocheted rug in front of the stove, but she heard what he said.

"If you think by being mean to Lady and to Grandma and me that you can solve your problem, you're wrong."

He stopped, leaned forward in his chair, and weighed his words.

"With us, it's like the trees. Grandma and I are the old oaks. You're the little pine. We'll be owning the forest for a while, and when the pines are big enough, they will." He waited. Jenny did not move at all.

"Change is not bad, Jenny. There will always be changes. But if you trust in God, you don't need to be afraid. God is the only one who never changes. Grandma and I can't always be with you. But Jesus will be—if you ask Him."

There was a long silence.

"Is that all?" Jenny asked.

"Yes," he said sadly.

Jenny turned away and went upstairs, closing the door against Lady.

In school the next day, Jenny was sullen. She wouldn't read aloud when it was her turn. She looked out the window during the math lesson until Mrs. Carson scolded her. And at recess she stayed in.

"What's wrong with you today, Jenny?" the teacher asked. "Are you getting sick?"

Jenny shook her head.

"What, then?"

"I just don't want to be out in the cold," Jenny said.

"Is that why you wouldn't read this morning?"

Jenny did not answer, and the teacher looked at her for a moment, and then went away.

When the buses came that afternoon, Jenny followed Teresa and Lynn to the bus.

"Hi, Jenny," Teresa, the older one, said.

"Hi," said Jenny.

"Are you getting on our bus?"

"Yes, I'm going to your house."

"You are?" Teresa was surprised, then suspicious. "Why?"

"I'm going to stay there."

"Are you sure?"

Jenny nodded.

Teresa did not look convinced. Lynn was delighted. But there was no arguing; the buses were ready to leave.

At the Stebbses' house, Mrs. Stebbs was watching television in the family room. Lynn and Teresa threw their coats on a kitchen chair.

"We're home," Lynn called.

"Hello, girls," a voice from the family room returned. "Get a popsicle if you want it."

"Want one?" Lynn asked Jenny.

"Sure." But she thought it was an odd thing to eat so close to supper.

"Mom," Teresa said, "Jenny came home with us."

Mrs. Stebbs appeared in the doorway of the family room.

"Jenny. Do the Logans know you're here?"

"Yes."

The woman looked puzzled.

Then she said, "Well, why don't you girls go in and watch T.V. Lynn, don't let that popsicle drip on the couch, do you hear?"

Even with the television on, Jenny could hear Mrs. Stebbs dialing the telephone in the kitchen. Her popsicle did not taste as good as she had thought it would. She could hear Mrs. Stebbs's voice clearly when the woman would turn from the counter to the stove.

"Um-hmn. I thought probably. Uh-huh. Oh, really? That's a shame. Yes, I see. What do you want me to do?"

"Jenny," Lynn said. "Do you want to watch a movie or a western?"

"I don't care," Jenny said quickly, trying not to miss what Mrs. Stebbs was saying in the kitchen.

"The movies are always boring. Let's watch a western."

"All right," Mrs. Stebbs said. "Let me call you back." She paused. "I know. You're welcome. Okay. Bye-bye." She hung up the phone.

"Jenny, would you come here, please?"

Jenny was relieved to hear that Mrs. Stebbs's voice had no anger in it.

She went to the kitchen, and she could feel Teresa and Lynn watching her from the doorway of the family room.

"I just talked to Mrs. Logan."

Jenny looked down at her shoes that still shone from the polishing Mr. Logan had given them.

"She told me why you ran away."

Jenny's cheeks burned. "I didn't run away. I was supposed to come here in the first place."

"I'm not going to argue with you. I'm going to call Mrs. McAllister and see what's to be done." She turned to the phone. "Go on in with the girls, now. I'll talk to you later."

Jenny started to leave.

"The Logans love you a lot, Jenny."

"They do not."

"Oh, Jenny. They do and you know it."

"I don't care." The old flatness had returned to her voice. "They're just old people."

Anger flickered in Mrs. Stebbs's eyes briefly. "You ought to have a licking for that."

Jenny's shoulder muscles tightened ever so slightly. Go ahead, she thought. But she had not had that sick feeling of fear for a long time that suddenly washed over her.

Mrs. Stebbs began to dial the phone. "Go on; I'll tell you what she says."

Jenny went back to the family room. But this time Mrs. Stebbs moved around the corner, and Jenny could not hear her words clearly.

It seemed like a long time later when Mrs. Stebbs came in carrying a tray.

"You girls can eat in here tonight. Daddy's not going to be here for a while."

It was hot dogs and lemonade and potato chips. Jenny liked the food, especially the lemonade. But it seemed as if there ought to be more kinds of things to eat. She sat by the couch, holding a paper plate and a glass. She tried to balance the plate on her knees. She began to feel lonely.

The news came on. Mrs. Stebbs ate a hot dog and watched some man telling how many homes had been destroyed in a flood. Jenny was totally bored, but she did not know where else to go. So she sat by the couch and waited for Lynn to finish eating. Lynn decided to eat another hot dog.

Jenny then waited for Mrs. Stebbs to finish with the news. What did Mrs. McAllister say, she wanted to know. She wished Mrs. Stebbs would tell her what was going to happen.

She looked around the room. There was a table at the other end of the room, stacked with games and magazines. Then there was a couch, a large brown plaid couch with buttons on the cushions. Behind her was the television. The walls and ceiling were painted beige; on the floor was green and brown shag carpeting. Somehow the room did not seem right to Jenny.

When Mrs. Stebbs began to fold clothes from the laundry basket on the end of the couch, Jenny finally asked, "What did she say?"

"She said for you not to worry. She will come out to see you in the morning." The lady snapped a towel out and folded it. "So tonight you can sleep in one of Lynn's nightgowns. We'll fix a mattress on the floor, okay? We don't have the other twin bed set up."

Jenny nodded. But somehow she did not feel any better.

Later that night, Jenny lay under a gold rayon blanket, listening to the strange sounds of a different house. Every few minutes the furnace would blow warm air through the vent just to Jenny's right. The pipes would clack, there would be a pause, and then the air would gush out with a roar. When the air wasn't on, she could hear Lynn's steady breathing. Finally she heard talking downstairs, and she knew Mr. Stebbs had come home. At first the voices were low; then they got louder. Jenny could hear no words, but she knew there was an argument. She had heard those tones in other houses. She felt sick and like she wanted to cry. Then the heat came on again and drowned out all other noises. It startled her every time it kicked on.

There had been nothing to do all evening. Teresa had done homework. Lynn had wanted to watch television. Because she was used to going outside after school, Jenny had asked to go out. Mrs. Stebbs had said, "Yes, but stay back from the street." There had been nothing to do out there either. She had walked down the drive to the streetlight, then come back and sat on the steps. She kicked the little snow that was left off the steps into the dead flowers along the walk. After a while she had gone back in to watch television.

"Is this what you always do?" she had asked Lynn.

"Mostly."

"Do you have a pet?"

"No. We had a cat once, but Mom didn't like the hair all over. It was a big white one with green eyes. Her name was Puff."

Jenny had listened wearily.

Now in the darkness, Jenny tried to fall asleep. She heard the Stebbses come upstairs. They were whispering now. Soon the house was completely quiet except for the furnace, and Jenny was awake all alone. Her eyes simply would not stay closed.

She considered going to Mrs. Stebbs, but she didn't know where her bedroom was. And she didn't really know what it was she would ask for anyway. She began to feel afraid in the strange room. It was as if the darkness had weight and were closing down on her.

Carefully, quietly, she got out of her covers, and tiptoed to the stairs. She listened, intently, and then went down, one cautious step at a time.

Light from a streetlight filled the front room with a milky dimness. Jenny sat down in the cushioned, high-back chair by the picture window, pulling her knees up in the circle of her arms. And only then did she start to cry.

At first just a few tears slid down one cheek. Then many came down both cheeks, and at last she was sobbing, shuddering as she drew her breath between sobs. She cried until her head ached and the nightgown over her knees was wet with tears. She cried until her breath came only in jerking gasps. She cried until she could cry no more.

When at last she could breathe more evenly, she laid her head back in the chair. She felt as if she had been running, all shaky and tired.

Jenny had been alone before. She had been afraid. She had been tired. But she had never been so lonely in her life. She had no idea what time it was. It was as if the night would go on forever, as if she were the only person in the world.

She looked out the window, up past the glow of the streetlight, past the bare, black limbs of a tree, to a few bright stars that shone on undiminished by the artificial light. Perhaps Mrs. Logan had looked at the stars tonight, too, Jenny thought. There was a sudden comfort in that thought. If she believed she could see the same stars as the Logans did, it seemed she were not so far away from them. She stared at the stars a long time.

After a while, though, the ache returned, heavy in her chest. It was unbearable. She felt as if she might cry out. And then she remembered what Mrs. Logan had said: "Jesus Christ, the same yesterday, today, and for ever." In a small, quivering voice, so small it barely disturbed the silence, Jenny said the words aloud. She looked out the window, through the trees again, to the stars. Suddenly the furnace turned on with a roar, and her tears came again.

Morning light spread gradually through the house, letting the rooms get brighter and brighter. It fell across the chair by the picture window where Jenny, bent forward on one of the arms, had been asleep for several hours. She woke up. Her cheeks were flushed and puffy, and her eyelids felt fat and numb. But she felt as if she had slept enough.

She remembered the verse Mrs. Logan had read, that she had repeated in the night. Suddenly she wanted to read it herself, see it on the page. She got up and looked around for a Bible. She finally found one on an end table in the family room, but even after much searching, she could not find the verse.

She heard an alarm clock go off somewhere upstairs and hurried back to her mattress and blankets before anyone had gotten up.

"Come on, girls. Lynn. Jenny." Mrs. Stebbs stood sleepily in the doorway. "Get up."

Jenny sat up and rubbed her eyes. Lynn stuck one leg out from under the blankets.

"Lynn, hurry up. Jenny, Mrs. McAllister said you should wait for her, and she'll take you to school. Okay? Lynn, honey, I'm not going to call you again, do you hear?"

Mrs. Stebbs went downstairs and started to make breakfast. Jenny and Lynn got dressed. Jenny folded her blankets up, putting her pillow on top.

The school bus came and went. Jenny sat in the kitchen with Mrs. Stebbs who still wore a terry cloth robe and slippers. At eight-thirty Mrs. McAllister pulled into the drive. Mrs. Stebbs went to the front door to meet her, and Jenny followed.

"Good morning," said Mrs. Stebbs.

"Good morning. Pretty cold this morning, isn't it?" Mrs. McAllister smiled and shivered.

"I haven't been out. My tolerance for cold is pretty low."

The women laughed together.

There was an awkward silence.

"Here's Jenny," Mrs. Stebbs said, finally.

"Yes. Good morning, Jenny."

"Good morning," said Jenny.

"How are you today?"

"Fine."

"Are you?" she asked, looking closely at the child. Then she took Jenny by the hand, and nodded at Mrs. Stebbs. Mrs. Stebbs went back to the kitchen and started to put the dishes in the dishwasher.

"Well, Jenny. What do you have to say?"

"I'm sorry. I really am."

"Well, that doesn't change anything, does it? Now running away to someone else's house is not the worst thing in the world. And if you were really the Logans' child, this would not be a major problem. But, honey, can you understand how it is with you? With you it's different."

Jenny looked steadily at the woman, her eyes bright. Mrs. McAllister studied her eyes.

"Have you been crying?"

Jenny dropped her gaze and nodded.

"Why did you cry?"

There was no answer for a long while.

"I think I was homesick."

Mrs. McAllister nearly cried herself. She said softly, "Oh, dear Jenny. Dear Jenny. Don't you know how it feels to be homesick? Have you never been homesick?"

Jenny did not know. "Nehemiah had a sad face and the king kept asking him if he was sick. He said, 'No, I want to go home.' And that's what I want. I just want to go home."

Mrs. McAllister leaned back and looked at the little girl. She sighed as though she had finished some difficult thing and now had to do it all over again.

"It's not so simple, I'm afraid," she said at last.

"I won't run away again. I like it there. Really."

Jenny's eyes pleaded with Mrs. McAllister.

"I'm not the one we have to convince." Again she sat a long time without saying anything. Finally she asked, "Do you *really* want to stay with the Logans?"

Jenny nodded.

"Really, Jenny? I mean it now."

"Yes," Jenny said, never taking her eyes from Mrs. McAllister's.

"What about the reason you left? Things haven't changed there, you know."

"I know. But I like it at the Logans."

"People don't run away from what they like."

Jenny blushed.

Mrs. McAllister went on. "How do you know you want to stay? How can I be sure you mean it?"

Jenny did not know what to say. She had thought that Mrs. McAllister would just drive her back to the Logans and that would be all there was to it.

"I just know I want to go. I want to go to the barn and I want to feed my calf and I want to eat at the table and have pie for dessert."

Mrs. McAllister continued to look down at her.

"And I want Grandma and Grandpa to find me something in the Bible. They know what is wrong with my heart."

The woman smiled faintly and rubbed her forehead. After a long silence she spoke.

"Get your coat, Jenny. I'll take you home."

9

THE ANTIQUE COLLECTOR

It snowed on and off during the whole next week. By Wednesday there was more than a foot of snow, a light, dry powder that swirled in the wind and drifted in arcs against buildings and fences. The great hemlocks around the Logans' house stood like white giants against the gray sky. On the birdfeeder outside the kitchen window, chickadees clustered, gobbling up sunflower seeds and suet as fast as Mr. Logan could carry the food out to them. It seemed to take Mrs. Logan longer to do the dishes now that the birdfeeder was up. Sometimes when she wasn't even washing the dishes, she stood at the sink to watch the cardinals and the many other birds that came.

It was snowing steadily the day Mrs. McAllister came. She left her boots on the porch and gladly took the rocker, holding her stocking feet up to the wood stove. Mrs. Logan offered her a cup of coffee, but the caseworker refused.

"I can't stay. But thanks. I just wanted to come tell you the latest in person."

Mr. and Mrs. Logan both sat quietly, waiting. Jenny sat on Mr. Logan's knee.

"I had another meeting with the director," the woman began. "Since our little problem last week"— at this Jenny lowered her eyes to the floor—"Mr. Wright has become more vocal. Says he told us something like this would happen." Mrs. McAllister shook her head. "He really means well. Really. I know he thinks he's doing what's best for Jenny."

Mr. Logan asked, "What does your director say?"

"Not much. I can't tell whether this case is beginning to intrigue him or frustrate him. But I've never seen him be anything but reasonable." She smiled faintly.

The old people waited still, letting her speak as she would.

"Anyway," she went on, "he wants to meet with you—to talk with you—on the twenty-third of this month."

"But," Mrs. Logan said, "that's so soon. We still have almost three months before the trial period is over."

Mrs. McAllister rocked her chair slightly.

"I don't know whether he plans to cut that short or what. But I feel sure that when he meets you, he'll give you your chance."

"Well, all right," Mr. Logan said. "Tell us what we should do."

"First of all, don't worry. How about if I call you later with the details? I need to find out what time for sure from his secretary. You can come, then, on the twenty-third?"

"We can," the old man said.

Later, as Mrs. McAllister drove away, Jenny watched the car as it disappeared beyond the hill. The snow came down thickly, like so many weary birds.

Please, Lord, thought Jenny, touching the cold glass of the window.

On Sunday the snow stopped falling, and the sun came up in a clear blue sky. Everywhere the snow sparkled, vast, rolling blankets of it that lay across whole fields, iced barns like so many cakes, and put peaked caps on pumps and posts. Jenny had never seen such unbroken splendor.

On Monday Jenny came home from school and found the Aladdin lamp in the middle of the kitchen table.

"Hi, Grandma. I'm home."

"Hello, honey." Mrs. Logan bent forward to kiss her but kept her floured hands on the rolling pin. "How was school?"

"Good. I got a hundred on my spelling words."

"Good for you." The old lady smiled proudly at Jenny. "What did you have for lunch?" she asked.

"Pizza."

"Oh, that's something you like. I've never made any of that. I don't think Grandpa would like it."

"He might," Jenny said, hopefully.

"Well, maybe we'll spring it on him sometime, then."

They giggled.

"Why is the lamp out here?" Jenny asked.

"The current went off a little while ago."

Jenny looked up at the clock over the sink. The second hand was not going around, and the time said three-fifteen.

"Oh, it did. Why is there no electricity?"

"Well, it goes off a lot in the winter. Snow and ice get on the lines up on the mountain. Pulls them down, I guess."

"What are we having for supper?"

"Pot roast," said Mrs. Logan.

"Oh, yea!"

"Do you mind setting the table before you go out? Chores might take a little longer tonight if you have to use lanterns."

"Okay. What kind of pie?"

"Chocolate."

"Yea!"

Jenny set the table, put on her barn clothes, and headed out.

"Tell Grandpa the current's off. He maybe doesn't know it yet," Mrs. Logan said.

"Okay, I will."

She went out into the gathering dimness of late afternoon. It was very quiet everywhere. She walked in the narrow path to the barn. Mr. Logan was not in where the cows were; so she went upstairs to the barn floor. He was sitting on grain bags in the huge open doorway, carving a piece of wood.

"Hi, Grandpa. Did you know the electricity is off?"

"Oh, is it? Well. Did you have a good day?"

"I got a hundred on my spelling."

"That's the stuff."

"Is that part of Grandma's mirror frame?"

He cocked his head and looked at her out of the corner of his eye. "How do you know what I'm making?"

"Grandma said you promised to make one. And this is the same kind of wood as the dresser. But I didn't say anything to Grandma."

He chuckled and kept carving. "Well, can't get anything past you, can I?"

"Will we use lanterns to do the milking?"

He glanced up at the horizon and then back at his work. "Probably."

He carved awhile more. Jenny sat by him and watched. At length he got up and went into the granary. When Jenny came in, he was putting the wood in a large wooden box. It was much darker in the granary. Her eyes adjusted to the dimness, and she saw Benjamin's harness on the walls. She walked over and ran her hands along the smooth reins.

"Where is Benjamin's halter?" she asked.

"On a peg downstairs."

"Can I have it?"

"What for?"

"I want to put it in my box in the attic."

He didn't answer right away. Finally he said, "No. I don't believe so. I think we should keep it right here in the barn where it belongs."

Jenny didn't say anything.

"Don't you think it belongs here?"

Jenny nodded without looking up. He waited, watching her. She looked up, then, and smiled at him.

"Okay."

"Okay," he said. "Now here's a lantern for you." He took two lanterns himself, and they went down to do the milking.

Jenny liked the warm light the lanterns made in the barn. It seemed cozy and close in there. The chewing of the cows and the sound of milk streaming into the pail were loud tonight.

"Will you be done with the frame in time for Christmas?" she asked.

"Most likely."

"I hope I'm here then."

"So do I."

"Do you think I will be?"

"I don't know, Jenny."

"When is that meeting with the man at the welfare?"

"Nine days," he said with an exactness unusual for him.

"Hello. Hello in there," a man's voice called from the door.

Mr. Logan got up and turned toward the door.

"Hello. What can I do for you?"

The man stepped inside the door, and the lantern by the wall lit up his face. Jenny did not know him. Apparently Mr. Logan didn't either.

"Are you lost?" Mr. Logan asked.

"Well, no," the man began. Then he noticed with interest the lantern to his right.

"Say, this is a pretty nice lantern. Old, isn't it?"

Mr. Logan leaned down to pick up his stool and pail. Jenny heard him sigh.

"You must be an antique dealer," he said.

"Sounds as if you might be tired of antique dealers."

"Well, they get pretty thick around here this time of year. They want to stock up for Christmas, I guess."

"Actually, I just collect antiques for myself. And I like nice lanterns. I hope that doesn't put me in a wrong category." He smiled pleasantly.

Mr. Logan smiled wryly. "I'm Nicholas Logan." He had come forward and put out his hand. He held both the pail and the stool with the other.

The stranger shook hands with him before he replied. "Hess. Peter Hess."

"Well, Mr. Hess, what can we do for you?"

The man grinned broadly.

"Would you want to sell me a lantern?"

"I'll tell you what I tell the others. We use everything we have. If we didn't use something, I'd certainly sell it to you." His voice was patient, friendly.

"Can't ever tell without asking, you know," said the other man.

"No harm in asking, young fellow."

"Don't let me hold up your work," the man said, motioning toward the cows.

"Just finished." Mr. Logan poured the last pail of milk through the strainer into the big, two-handled can and pushed the lid on. "Just looking for antiques, are you?"

"Yes. Antiques." He smiled a curious smile that Jenny did not understand.

As Mr. Logan carried the can into the milkhouse, he picked up his gloves from the stone ledge.

"You'd be welcome to stay for supper. We're just going in," he said as he passed Mr. Hess.

The man looked surprised. "Oh, thank you very much. That's very kind of you. But I just saw lights in your barn here and thought I'd stop. Do you always use lanterns?"

"No. The current's off."

"Oh, I see."

Mr. Logan turned to Jenny. "Are you ready to go?"

"Yes," she said, coming out of Millie's stanchion.

"Blow out your lantern then. We'll just take this one. Now, young fellow, why don't you come in to supper? It's always nice to have company for supper."

"Well," the man hesitated.

"Yes, come along," said the farmer. Jenny was now standing beside Mr. Logan. She reached up and took the old man's hand. "This is Jenny."

"Hello, Jenny."

"Hello," she said with a bashful glance.

As the three walked to the house, Jenny watched the lantern spread a gold circle on the snow. It opened the darkness for some distance ahead of them.

Mrs. Logan had already pulled the table out from the wall and set a fourth place, Jenny immediately saw as she entered the kitchen. Lady got up from the rug by the stove and came forward. Jenny hugged her around the neck.

"Eda, this is Mr. Hess."

"Pleased to meet you," she said. "I saw you drive in, and I thought Nicholas would bring you to supper."

"I hope it's no trouble, Mrs. Logan. I really did not expect to invite myself to dinner."

"I'm sure you didn't invite yourself. We love to have company." Her smile was real. She took his coat and handed it to Mr. Logan.

"Thank you very much." The young man's eyes were drawn to the bright lamp on the table. "Oh! This is in beautiful condition." He stopped and glanced at Mr. Logan. "I'm sorry. I'm at it again, aren't I?"

"Are you a dealer?" Mrs. Logan asked, putting a platter of pot roast on the table.

"Oh, no," he said quickly.

"He thinks I shoot antique dealers," Mr. Logan told his wife.

She laughed and then indicated which chair was to be for Mr. Hess. "Nicholas doesn't shoot them, but we have one for dinner now and then."

They all laughed then, as they pulled their chairs up to the table.

"Jenny, it's your turn to say the blessing," Mr. Logan said.

She looked across the table shyly at Mr. Hess and then at Mr. Logan. The old man winked at her, and she bowed her head.

"Heavenly Father, thank you for this day and for this house. Thank you for helping me with my spelling. Please bless this pot roast and the pie that's coming. Amen."

Mr. Hess was grinning as the others raised their heads. Mr. Logan had an amused twinkle in his eye. But neither of them made any comment.

"What business are you in, Mr. Hess?" asked Mrs. Logan, passing him the platter.

"Well, I used to be the manager of a grocery store, but now I work for the government."

"Tax department?" Mr. Logan asked with a grin.

"Oh, no. Though I think I wouldn't tell you if I were. You'd have me for dinner for sure then."

The Logans laughed.

"What do you do, Mr. Logan? Farm, I can see," the man said.

"Yes, farm some. I do a little logging too. I used to be a carpenter."

"He still is," Mrs. Logan put in.

"Really? Houses or cabinets?" The stranger looked back to Mr. Logan.

"Both," said Mr. Logan without boastfulness.

The conversation turned to other things and eventually came around to Jenny.

"This sure is a pretty granddaughter you have," said Mr. Hess.

"Thank you," said Mr. Logan.

Mrs. Logan smiled and patted Jenny's hand. Jenny smiled and looked up.

"I'm not really their granddaughter. I just live here." The statement was one of simple honesty, without embarrassment or resentment.

"Oh," was all the man said.

"She has a different last name, but that's about the only thing," Mrs. Logan said.

The man looked at Mr. Logan as if he didn't know what he should say.

The old man rescued him. "Jenny's staying with us on sort of a trial basis. The welfare people aren't sure we're young enough to deserve her."

"Oh, I see."

"We'll know pretty soon," Jenny said.

"We have to meet with the officials in a few days, and then we'll know if Jenny can stay or not," Mr. Logan explained.

"Well, I'm sure they'll see what fine people you are."

There was a pause.

Mr. Hess looked at Mr. Logan. "At least that's one good thing about antique dealers. They know that age adds value to things."

Mr. Logan chuckled. "Well, that's so. But only if the thing was good to begin with."

The topic was too important to Jenny to let it drop.

"They just have to let me stay," she said.

"Would you like more corn, Mr. Hess?" Mrs. Logan asked.

"No, thank you. I couldn't. You are a wonderful cook, Mrs. Logan."

"Well, thank you. You picked a good night to come. We don't always have pot roast on a weekday."

After pie and coffee, Jenny and Mrs. Logan cleared the table. They put the dishes on the drain board but did not wash them.

"Would you like to sit in the other room?" Mr. Logan asked Mr. Hess. "I could build a fire in the fireplace in no time."

"Actually I prefer the kitchen."

Mr. Logan smiled and nodded. They continued to sit at the empty table. Mrs. Logan came back and sat at the table too. Jenny sat by the stove with Lady.

"Is the electricity's being off much of a bother?" Mr. Hess asked.

"Not much. We just have to remember to strike a match instead of flip a switch. With the wood stove and all, life goes on pretty much the same," Mr. Logan said.

"Except," Mrs. Logan said, looking at her husband, "we have to pump the water from the well."

"Oh, yes. Do you need some pumped, Eda?"

"Sometime tonight."

"Oh, let me get the water. Really, it's the least I can do. I mean, after all, you gave me a meal that I couldn't have afforded in a restaurant," Mr. Hess said.

"Oh, no. I'll get it later," said Mr. Logan.

"No, really. Let me."

Mr. Hess was allowed to pump the water. Jenny watched him through the back door. He pumped vigorously, lifting the red handle up and shoving it down almost joyously. He brought two pails in and set them carefully by the stove.

"Thank you," said Mrs. Logan.

"I had forgotten what fun it is to pump water. I haven't done it since I was a boy. My uncle had a pump on his farm."

"Not too many people have them any more," Mr. Logan said.

"It's a shame, too. Everyone should have to pump water at least once," Mr. Hess said. He brushed his hands together as if they might have gotten dusty. "I really should be going. I have a rather long drive."

"Well, we'd like you to stay a while," Mr. Logan said.

"Thank you. I'd like to, but I should get going. Jenny, I hope you get to stay here. It's a good place, isn't it?"

"Yes, sir."

"Well, I'm sure everything will work out." He smiled pleasantly.

"It would if I hadn't run away," Jenny said.

"That's all, Jenny," Mrs. Logan said quickly. "Mr. Hess doesn't want to hear all our troubles."

He looked at Mr. Logan, then at Mrs. Logan. "That's all right. Really."

Jenny was desperate to explain. "I didn't want things to change. But Grandpa says things always change. Except God. God never changes."

No one said anything for a few seconds.

Mr. Logan looked at Mr. Hess. "Christ promises never to leave or forsake anyone who believes in Him."

"Seems a good thing to believe," Mr. Hess finally said. "Well, thank you again, Mr. Logan. Mrs. Logan. It certainly has been a pleasure."

Mr. Logan walked Mr. Hess to his car with a lantern. Jenny stayed on the back porch, watching them.

The young man said, "This may be, of course, none of my business, but I think you may damage your chances of keeping the little girl if you talk too much about God. Or if she does. Believe me. I work in a government office. I know how they think." His voice carried well in the still winter air, but he did not realize it.

"Well," said Mr. Logan slowly, "I can't see teaching Jenny one thing and doing another myself. I believe we'll just go on as we have been. Not that I take your intent amiss. I know you mean well by it. But you cannot leave God out of anything and win."

"You really believe that, don't you, Mr. Logan?"

"I do."

Mr. Logan still held the lantern forth, his clean features lit by it. The young man looked thoughtful, and then reached for his car door. "Well, if you won't take my advice, will you take my money? I really would like to have that Aladdin lamp you've got. It's a beauty. Name your price."

"Sorry, Mr. Hess. We're still using it."

"Well, you never know until you ask."

"No harm in asking, young fellow," said Mr. Logan pleasantly. "Stop by again."

Just before bedtime that evening Jenny got up in Mr. Logan's lap. She twirled her hair around her finger for some time before she spoke.

"That man doesn't believe in God, does he?" she said at last. "Like we do."

"I don't think so," he said.

She put her head against his shoulder.

"Should I not tell the welfare people about God?"

Mr. Logan thought a minute. "Did Nehemiah forget God when he went to the king?"

"No."

"Well, then."

10

THE DECISION

The electricity was still off the next morning. Mrs. Logan heated water for Jenny on the stove, and the little girl washed her face in a basin.

"This is the way we always used to wash," Mrs. Logan said.

"It's fun," Jenny said.

"Um-hmm," was all Mrs. Logan said.

The current came back on that afternoon.

It got warmer during the next two days, and much of the snow melted. Then it turned cold again, the wind whistling through the hemlocks and the house snapping in the night.

Mr. Logan stomped in from morning chores. His nose and cheeks were red. Lady's fur was like ice to touch.

"It's a blinger out there this morning," he said.

Mrs. Logan called up through the register for Jenny to dress "plenty warm."

The next day it was a little warmer, and the following day it snowed, big, wet flakes that stuck to the frozen ground and piled up fast. Jenny watched through the kitchen window as it pelted down.

"Will school be called off?" she asked.

"I don't think so," Mrs. Logan answered. And it wasn't.

When Jenny came home from school, there were six to seven inches on the ground. It was a beautiful thick snow.

Mrs. Logan was singing in the kitchen when Jenny came. She could hear the rich voice before she even

opened the porch door. She knew the tune from church—"Great Is Thy Faithfulness."

She swung the door open. "Hi, Grandma. I'm home."

"Hello, honey."

Mrs. Logan was pouring a big bowl of creamy liquid into a metal cylinder. Beside her on the floor was a large wooden bucket and a steel handle.

"What are you doing?" Jenny asked.

"Why, we're going to have a little ice cream tonight."

Jenny's eyes opened wide. "You can make your own ice cream?"

"We sure can. I mix it up, and you and Grandpa crank it. That's fair, isn't it?"

"I guess so."

Mrs. Logan laughed as if she knew something Jenny didn't. She kissed her on the top of the head and then said, "Wait until it's cranked and then tell me."

Mr. Logan did most of the cranking. It seemed to take a long time. Jenny sat on the porch with him and carried in pans of snow once in a while.

But, oh, the eating of it was wonderful. It was much colder than store-bought ice cream, and lighter. The rich vanilla made Jenny close her eyes with pleasure at every bite. She ate two bowlfuls of the wonderful stuff and sat back satisfied.

She had no homework, and so she asked Mr. Logan to play checkers.

Jenny and Mr. Logan sat silently studying the game board. She concentrated, taking a long time to make her moves. She would reach for a checker and then draw her hand back. She tried to think through what would happen from all directions if she moved her checker a certain way.

At last they both had only two checkers apiece left. After much study, she finally moved her king forward. Mr. Logan smiled at her.

"Well, you've got me," he said.

"I do?" She gazed at the board in wonder.

"In two moves, I'll be done for." He seemed happy to be losing, she thought.

And indeed Jenny did win. She had thought she would have been happier when she finally won a game. Instead she felt a little sorry. She was, nonetheless, surprised.

"Did you let me win?" she asked.

Mr. Logan sat back and looked steadily at her. "I would not make your win so cheap as that."

She did not understand all that he meant by that, but she understood that she had won, and fairly.

They put away the game, and Jenny went to sit on the floor by Lady. She stroked the dog's ears gently.

Jenny knew without asking that it was just two more days until the meeting with the welfare officials. She wished it were farther away.

"What if they won't let me stay here?" There was a tightness in her voice she could not hide.

"That's something we have to think about," Mr. Logan said.

Mrs. Logan put down the sock she was mending. "You will get another home then, Jenny. And you will have to be good about it and get to like it."

"But I don't want another home." Jenny could barely hold back the tears.

"And we don't want you to have one either." The old man's voice was low and thick. "But if they say you must go, you must."

Jenny didn't see how she could stand it. She gathered Lady to her and pushed her face into the furry neck.

"But remember, wherever you go, God is there." Mr. Logan's voice was calm.

Jenny's throat ached, and her head pounded from holding in her crying. Finally she managed to nod.

"If it were the Lord's plan for you to be somewhere else, you must believe it's for the good. It means He has something better for you, even if it doesn't seem so at first."

In a little while she said, "I'm going to tell them about the trees—how you are the oaks and I am the pine."

"You can tell them that," he said. "But I want you to remember that whether the oaks fall or stand . . . ." He waited for her to finish his sentence.

"God is there," she said solemnly.

He nodded once, with a finality and a surety.

The morning of the meeting, Jenny woke long before she was called. In the faint early morning light she looked at the picture of the Logan family on the wall at the foot of her bed. She could not remember being in a picture with anyone in her whole life.

When Mrs. Logan called her, she got out of bed and stood over the register. She and Mrs. Logan had decided the night before that she should wear the burgundy corduroy skirt and vest. The outfit lay over the chair. Jenny looked at it as she stood over the grating, the warm air billowing out her nightgown. The vest with its pocket hanky that matched the blouse was Jenny's favorite thing to wear.

Soon she got dressed, but she did not brush her hair. Instead she carried the brush and two barrettes down to Mrs. Logan, who pulled her hair back on each side and combed it straight in the back.

"You look mighty pretty," said the old lady. She held up a hand mirror for Jenny. The image before her pleased the little girl.

"So do you," she told Mrs. Logan.

Mrs. Logan was wearing her Sunday dress and pearls. "It's more like a Sunday than a Wednesday, isn't it?"

"Where is Grandpa?" Jenny asked.

"Up changing his clothes."

Then Jenny heard his familiar step on the stairs. He came into the kitchen in his winter suit, carrying his hat. Jenny thought how handsome he was in his blue-gray suit.

Mr. Logan said a blessing over breakfast that took in the weather, the trip, the farm, Jenny, the meeting, and finally the food.

Breakfast was quiet. Jenny could not seem to taste her shredded wheat. At last, she gave up trying to eat it. Mrs. Logan said nothing to her about wasting food.

Things were even quieter in the car. They passed Jacob in his truck. The Logans waved to him. When they went past the Meyers's, Marion was out by the mailbox putting letters in. She clutched her sweater closed with one hand and waved with the other. They all waved back.

Eventually Jenny could see her school ahead. They were going to meet Mrs. McAllister there. They would all go to town together. She felt as if she might be sick.

Mr. Logan pulled in at the school and put the car in park. Jenny looked at the tracks the buses had made earlier. Mrs. McAllister appeared on the porch, and Jenny noticed that the woman's coat wasn't buttoned and she carried no purse.

As she came toward their car, Mr. Logan turned off the engine and rolled down his window.

"Good morning," the lady said. Her breath went out in a white cloud before her lips.

"Morning," Mr. Logan said and smiled at her.

"I tried to catch you before you left. I must have just missed you."

Mr. Logan and his wife waited for her to go on with their usual unhurried patience.

"The director called me earlier. He said for you not to bother coming in to town."

Mr. Logan's smile faded. Mrs. Logan bit her lower lip. Jenny neither moved nor changed her expression.

"Well, that's it, then," the old man said.

"No, no. You misunderstand," Mrs. McAllister said, reaching through the window and touching his shoulder lightly. "He said you should keep Jenny. He decided that an interview wasn't necessary."

She was smiling. Mrs. Logan's eyes brimmed with tears, and Mr. Logan blinked several times. Mrs. Logan reached back for Jenny's hand.

"I can't believe it," the man said.

"I can't either, to tell you the truth," the lady said, putting her hands under her arms because she was starting to get cold. "Has anyone from the office been out to your house?"

"No." Mr. Logan looked at Mrs. Logan, and she shook her head.

"Well, I didn't think so. But Mr. Hess said to be sure to tell you that if you get so you don't use your Aladdin lamp anymore, he would really like to buy it."

"Ah," said Mrs. Logan. "Mr. Hess."

All the old man said was, "So the king came to Nehemiah this time."

"What?" Mrs. McAllister tilted her head.

"Oh, Jenny thought she was like Nehemiah going to the king. Your Mr. Hess. He did come one evening, and I thought he was an antique dealer."

"Well, what do you know," Mrs. McAllister said.

They all were quiet for a moment.

"I'll be out now and again to see you folks," the caseworker said. "In fact I'll be out in a day or two with the papers. There are always papers to sign, you know—to make you legal and all. And Mr. Hess said he'd like to talk to you sometime, Mr. Logan." She smiled warmly. "I can't tell you how glad I am this all worked out."

"Thank you for all your help," Mr. Logan said.

"Yes. A thousand thanks," Mrs. Logan said.

Mrs. McAllister looked at Jenny. The little girl was smiling so broadly that she seemed to shine.

"That's thanks enough," said Mrs. McAllister.

They said good-bye and Mrs. McAllister walked back toward the school. Mr. Logan rolled up his window and looked at Jenny in the rear-view mirror.

"Looks like you're stuck with us," he said.

She could not stop grinning.

"Well, Nicholas," Mrs. Logan said, "we're mighty dressed up to be just going home."

He looked at her with one of his crooked smiles. "And what do you have in mind?"

"I thought we all might have a picture made. Jim would probably take us without an appointment."

Mr. Logan thought it over. "You're right. We shouldn't waste our good looks."

He turned on the engine. "Is that all right with you, Jenny Wren?"

She nodded, still smiling.

"And then will we go home?" she asked.

"And then we'll go home," he said, backing out of the school lot and pulling onto the road.

All along the road, pines and leafless trees held up fresh snow to the morning sun. Jenny thought the trees had never looked more beautiful.